THE SUCCESSFUL MIDDLE SCHOOL COUNSELING PROGRAM

ELISE KENNEY-CALDWELL AND
ANN MCCARTY PEREZ, ED.D.

Copyright © by the Association for Middle Level Education. All rights reserved.

Pages labeled with the statement: **Copyright © 2023 by the Association for Middle Level Education. All rights reserved** are intended for reproduction. Permission is hereby granted to the purchaser of one copy of The Successful Middle School Counseling Program to reproduce these pages in sufficient quantity only for meeting the purchaser's own non-commercial educational needs.

No other part of this publication may be reproduced or transmitted in any form or by any means, electronic or mechanical, without permission in writing from the publisher except in the case of brief quotations embodied in reviews or articles.

AMLE, The Successful Middle School, and This We Believe are registered trademarks of the Association for Middle Level Education.

Printed in the United States of America

ISBN: 978-1-56090-009-2

Library of Congress Control Number: 2023944458

Why this book and why now?

The global pandemic of 2020 will have ripple effects for years. As this book is being published, schools are struggling through a national teacher and substitute shortage, an adolescent mental health crisis, low staff morale, and the continuing academic impacts of interrupted learning. While the role of the school counselor has grown and adapted to meet these changing needs, many school leaders might be operating from a dated understanding of the school counselor's role in schools.

The uniqueness of middle school counseling helps to bridge the time between childhood and young adulthood. At no other time outside of birth through age three does the brain develop as rapidly as during the middle school years, making a holistic approach to meeting the needs of students essential. Middle school counselors are invaluable in meeting those unique needs, using their specific training and expertise to help school staff bridge the gap of independence with the need for scaffolding.

By combining our wisdom and experience, we hope to help you understand the important role of comprehensive counseling services in middle schools and how to best utilize the resources you have.

INTRODUCTION

We have always known that school counselors are important, but can most of us articulate what they do on a daily basis? Based on a combined 50+ years in education, your authors believe that not all can. In fact, we still often hear them referred to as guidance counselors (more on why that is not a preferred title later). Hosting informational meetings about how to fill out your FAFSA is no longer the role of

THE SUCCESSFUL MIDDLE SCHOOL COUNSELING PROGRAM

school counselor. Instead, it is an all-encompassing role charged with meeting the ever-expanding needs of students and school staff. The role of a professional school counselor has become increasingly more complex and necessary as the needs of schools change. In the same way, our understanding of their importance to schools must also evolve. The Association for Middle Level Education (AMLE)'s Characteristics of Successful Middle Schools have included reference to comprehensive counseling services since the first edition of the text was published in 1982 as *This We Believe*. In 2003, the American School Counselor Association (ASCA) published the ASCA National Model, acknowledging that counseling's 100-plus-year history had evolved from "a position, to a service, to a program," which laid the foundation for its organizational concept in the model. By exploring these foundational documents, we gain a better understanding of the intricacies and demands of comprehensive school counseling services and how we can best meet the needs of young adolescents through collaboration and execution.

With rapid changes in growth and development, hormone fluctuations, and an underdeveloped frontal cortex, we know that middle school can sometimes be a wild ride. We're inviting you to take this ride on our steam engine train. Together, we will consider the intricacies of the rail system (or school counseling program, in our metaphor) and how they work efficiently together to move goods and passengers across the world. Each section of this book will help you visualize this middle school transportation system and how every part is necessary to keep the train moving.

We encourage you to approach this journey with vulnerability and an open mind with the hope that you see new or different approaches to serving your students. As educators we are tasked with serving the whole child. This book will help you do that by harnessing the power of all staff to do the right things, not more things. This book is written with collaboration and reflection in mind. The activities are designed for administrators, counselors, or any school staff to use to evaluate current practices and understand how the role of the school counseling program is not separate, but an integral part of the school. Brené Brown says it best in her book *Daring to Lead*:

Why this book and why now?

"a leader is anyone who takes responsibility for finding the potential in people and processes, and who has the courage to develop that potential."

THE SUCCESSFUL MIDDLE SCHOOL: THIS WE BELIEVE

The fifth edition of AMLE's foundational text, *The Successful Middle School: This We Believe,* describes the ideal middle school as one built around Essential Attributes. These Essential Attributes "can be realized and achieved best through the 18 Characteristics, which are grouped into three categories: Culture and Community; Curriculum, Instruction, and Assessment; and Leadership and Organization." *The Successful Middle School Counseling Program* is a companion guide which serves to help middle grades educators explore the intricacies of the school counselor role and how the Essential Attributes and 18 Characteristics offer lenses through which to see your school counseling program. Ideas and strategies for school counseling programs are tied to *The Successful Middle School: This We Believe* and linked to research and best practice.

ABOUT THIS BOOK

This book outlines recommended components of comprehensive middle school counseling services to best meet the ever-changing needs of young adolescents. It can be used by school communities to help implement all or portions of the middle school philosophy and comprehensive school counseling services to embrace the 18 Characteristics of Successful Middle Schools.

This book is divided into three sections that will help your team better understand the role of a counseling program in schools, foundational pieces, and how to implement a Comprehensive School Counseling Program. Included in the various sections are activities and templates that you can use with your staff, students, or families to ensure that you are providing comprehensive school counseling services. Along the way, you'll find "Principal Perspectives" in response to the question, "What was something you either learned or wish you had known about the school counseling program in your first year as principal?" Additionally, you will also see "Counselor Call Ins" that provide voice from current school counselors answering, "What do you wish school administrators practiced?"

In Section One, we will define what it means to have a comprehensive school counseling program and highlight the various roles within schools that are important to its success. This section will help you audit your current program and identify opportunities for improvement.

In Section Two, we explore some of the foundational frameworks that shape school counseling programs. The literature is vast on serving students; we will pull them all together to help you realize how meeting the many needs of young adolescents is all connected.

In Section Three, we explore the unique aspects of middle schools and how to leverage that knowledge to maximize your school counseling program's effectiveness. You will better understand how to facilitate collaboration between school counselors and other staff to the benefit of students.

Contents

SECTION 1: The Who
"The Train Depot"
Definition, Roles, and Importance of Comprehensive School Counseling Programs
1

1	Defining Comprehensive School Counseling Programs	4
2	The Role of School Counselors	7
3	The Role of School Administrators	10
4	The Role of Teachers	13
5	The Role of Families	15
6	The Role of Community	19
7	The Role of Students Voice	20

SECTION 2: The What
"The Middle School Transportation System"
Foundational Documents and Frameworks for Comprehensive Services
25

8	Rail 1: Essential Attributes and the 18 Characteristics	28
9	Rail 2: The American School Counseling Association (ASCA) National Model	38
10	Rail Ties: Social-Emotional Learning (SEL) and the Collaborative for Academic, Social, and Emotional Learning (CASEL) Framework	50

| 11 | The Engine: Multi-Tiered Systems of Support | 60 |
| 12 | Bringing It All Together: The Train is Leaving the Station | 68 |

SECTION 3: The How
"All aboard!"
Systematic Approach to Programming and Implementation

71

13	Defining the Systematic Approach in Comprehensive School Counseling Programs	73
14	The School Advisory Program	78
15	The Team Approach	81
16	Connecting Everything: Working Smarter	95

CONCLUSION	101
APPENDIX LIST	107
ABOUT THE AUTHORS	121
REFERENCES	125

Glossary of Terms

In supporting the reader's navigation, the authors have provided definitions of key terms as they are used throughout the text. For a more complete list of middle level education-related terms, consider consulting AMLE's Middle School Glossary, available at https://amle.org/SMS.

Advisory: Regularly scheduled times when young adolescents have the opportunity to interact with a small group of peers and a teacher-advisor to discuss school and personal concerns. The group may be grade level or multi-grade level. In many schools advisors and their students remain together for three years.

Advisory Council: A structure of the Comprehensive School Counseling Program that allows a representative group of school and community stakeholders to inform programming and communicate and advocate for program goals.

The ASCA National Model: Outlines the components of a school counseling program that is integral to the school's academic mission and is created to have a significant positive impact on student achievement, attendance and discipline.

ASCA Mindsets and Behaviors: Describe the knowledge, skills and attitudes students need to achieve academic success, college and career readiness, and social/emotional development.

Collaborative Team: Teams of two or more teachers who share the same content, sometimes referred to as professional learning communities (PLCs).

The Successful Middle School Counseling Program

Comprehensive School Counseling Program (CSCP): The sum of programs and services provided by the professional school counseling staff in alignment with the American School Counselor Association (ASCA) National Model.

Consultative Services: The process by which the school counselor works with parents, teachers, administrators, and other stakeholder to effect positive change for a student.

Direct School Counseling Services: Includes any time that a school counselor is interacting directly with a student. This could be through individual counseling, small group, classroom lessons, or large group instruction.

Educational Equity: Takes into consideration the fact that the social identifiers (race, gender, socioeconomic status, etc.) do, in fact, affect equality. In an equitable environment, an individual or a group would be given what was needed to give them equal advantage. This would not necessarily be equal to what others receive. It could be more or different, ensuring that everyone has the resources they need to succeed.

Indirect School Counseling Services: Is time spent not directly with students, but instead in activities that support student growth and needs. Indirect services can include, but are not limited to, parent meetings, teacher consultation, and student support meetings.

Interdisciplinary Team: Teams of two to five teachers representing the core subjects. The team shares the same schedule, students, area of the building, responsibility for the core courses, and has common planning time.

Middle School Model: A school that has been planned and organized to address the developmental and cultural needs of students of ages 10 to 14, and that generally includes grades 5 through 8, although many varied patterns exist. For example, a school might include only grades 7 and 8 and still be called a middle school.

Multi-Tiered Systems of Support: An umbrella term that describes a variety of services provided in schools that considers the intensity and frequency with

Glossary of Terms

which they are delivered. It anticipates a systematic approach that includes intervention for academics and behaviors as well as a framework for pedagogy, leadership, professional learning, equitable access, and implementation.

Needs Assessment: A form of perception data. This survey could contain questions asked in a variety of formats, including using a Likert scale, offering a list of topics to select from, etc.

Outcome Data: Demonstrates the CSCP's effect on a common goal of school improvement.

Perception Data: Obtains stakeholder voice and feedback on what knowledge was gained as a result of a school counselor intervention or activity. This might include needs assessments, exit tickets, etc.

Process Data: Highlights how many students are reached as a result of the CSCP or the success of a program or process implemented by the CSCP team.

Social-Emotional Learning (SEL): As defined by Collaborative for Academic, Social, and Emotional Learning (CASEL), SEL the process through which all young people and adults acquire and apply the knowledge, skills, and attitudes to develop healthy identities, manage emotions and achieve personal and collective goals, feel and show empathy for others, establish and maintain supportive relationships, and make responsible and caring decisions.

Whole Child: Addressing the needs of students honoring and nurturing all aspects of the student as a whole human being ensuring that healthy, safe, engaged, supported, and challenged.

Section One

The Who

Section One

The Who
"The Train Depot"

DEFINITION, ROLES, AND IMPORTANCE OF COMPREHENSIVE SCHOOL COUNSELING PROGRAMS

To begin, we ask you to visualize an aerial view of a train station. Trains come and go from multiple destinations, a variety of buildings serve many purposes, and people are working in several roles as passengers make their way to their platform. Each part of the depot supports the greater purpose of transportation. As you continue through this section, remember that view and how each group mentioned is integral to that purpose.

CHAPTER 1: DEFINING COMPREHENSIVE SCHOOL COUNSELING PROGRAMS

The Successful Middle School: This We Believe
Characteristics Crossover

- Policies and practices are student centered, unbiased, and fairly implemented.
- Leaders are committed to and knowledgeable about young adolescents, equitable practices, and educational research.
- A shared vision developed by all stakeholders guides every decision.

Definitions of comprehensive school counseling may differ based on the person's experience in school. We will begin with technical definitions and then offer our best descriptions, which should help you to better understand our experience and why we're passionate about middle school counseling.

ASCA articulates that, "Comprehensive School Counseling Programs are developed, delivered, and maintained to promote students' achievement in academic, career, and personal and social domains." The framework of a school counseling program consists of four components:

- define,
- manage,
- deliver, and
- assess.

Programs include both direct and indirect services that are accessed by students and other school stakeholders both in and out of the classroom. First introduced in 2003, ASCA's framework has evolved to support professional school counselors in providing consistent levels of support for all students, while allowing for the flexibility to adapt their programs to align with building vision and mission statements (See *The Successful Middle School Schedule* for more activities on creating a middle school vision and mission).

As schools **DEFINE** their Comprehensive School Counseling Program (CSCP), ensuring that program activities address developmentally appropriate mindsets and behaviors of all students will be a key to success.[1] Each year, this component should include a beginning-of-year meeting with the school leadership team to set clear expectations for the school counselor role, as well as allow for the principal to have voice and insight into goals for student growth for the year. Lastly, school counselors should use a backward design process to plan the year's activities, including classroom guidance or advisory lesson plans, small counseling groups, and other school-wide initiatives.

To **MANAGE** their CSCP, school counselors should identify program goals that align with school improvement goals for the year. The CSCP should support school-wide multi-tiered systems of support (MTSS) efforts through its programming and varying levels of service. This includes using data to identify interventions that address student needs at each tier. Collaboration with other MTSS stakeholders will better address the needs and growth of the whole child.

To **DELIVER** the CSCP, building leadership can put structures and appropriate expectations in place to support the recommended minimum of 80% of counselors' time to be served in direct and indirect services.[2] When creating the school schedule, it is important that administrators consider programmatic needs in order to provide time and space for delivery.[3] Because this is the bulk of their daily work, clearly defining counseling programming helps communicate "what school counselors do" to the rest of the staff. The ASCA National Model provides data collection tools for school counselor time analysis. Using these tools will help define the effectiveness of time spent by school counselors providing different levels of support across stakeholder groups.

Finally, schools should **ASSESS** their practices to ensure they are fulfilling their intended purpose. The assess phase considers cause and effect data by looking at both implementation and impact on students. Assessing practices helps determine the effectiveness of the program as well as provide insight into what may need to be changed or added. It is also an opportunity for collaboration where school counselors can contribute to evidence of improvement in school plans.

What is Comprehensive School Counseling? The Experts' View

To start this book journey, we first wanted to provide our own definitions of comprehensive school counseling. Our colleague Debbie Ondrus lent us her definition as well. You could consider these our CSCP elevator pitches.

How many times have we heard or said to ourselves, "I would never go back to middle school!" Yes, this time in life can be challenging. But why do we "awfulize" it so? We believe that we can change the narrative by ensuring schools have enough tools in their toolbox to help middle schoolers manage this critical developmental phase. When a school has a strong CSCP, not only do students develop tools, adults around them equally benefit from picking up a few tricks along the way.

– Elise Kenney-Caldwell, author and middle school counselor

When I think of the term Comprehensive School Counseling Program, the first words that come to mind are "whole child." But what does that really mean? It means addressing a variety of needs that include social-emotional, academic, decision making, and thinking about the future—and not necessarily in that order. I think of the program as the family room of the school. Everyone is welcome and should be comfortable. It is the school's heartbeat and counselors have a finger on the pulse. The CSCP helps to round out the experience of students and ensure their needs are met.

– Ann McCarty Perez, author, consultant and former middle school principal and teacher

School counseling expands across all areas of the school setting from school-wide programming, classroom instruction, targeted small groups, community correspondence, and more! School counselors are able to see the big picture of what the students experience which drives them to advocate for them and bring valuable resources to the table during closing-the-gap action planning. A school counseling program is not by chance; it is developed over time through increased awareness of the school counselor competencies and standards, as well as professional conversations and collaboration. We want to work together – not in silos – to create the best opportunities for the students.

– Debbie Ondrus, community outreach & student wellness coordinator, former middle school counselor

The Who: "The Train Depot"

Expert Advice: The middle school concept intertwines many roles, including school counselors, administrators, teachers, families, community, and students, and clear definitions are often difficult. In this section, we will define how each role, while working within the school, can specifically support the efforts of the CSCP.

CHAPTER 2: THE ROLE OF SCHOOL COUNSELORS

The Successful Middle School: This We Believe
Characteristics Crossover

- Comprehensive counseling and support services meet the needs of young adolescents.

> **COUNSELOR CALL IN**
>
> The role of the school counselor can be complex. We are not only the trusted adult for students but a support for the administrators, staff and community members which can drain away from our personal well-being. Self-care is important in this profession and counselors need to have time to refocus during the day.
>
> -Gretchen Brenckle

If you ever want to see a professional school counselor flinch, call them a "guidance" counselor. Why? The school counselor role has evolved far beyond its historic roots of preparing transcripts and helping students with scholarships; now, school counselors not only assist students with academic, social-emotional, and career needs but also support adults. Furthermore, the media has not helped in its portrayal of school counselors. Typical teen comedies often show a loopy school counselor who can't seem to get it right; consider the implications this has for the actual and important work of professional school counselors. It is critical for school counselors to help reshape this image and educate school staff on the "real work" of CSCPs.

Perceptions vs. Reality Exercise

In the chart below, have staff write down their assumptions about the school counselor role. Then, have staff answer the questions about a school counselor's responsibilities and how much time they should spend attending to each. When finished, compare answers with the school counselor.

Assumptions about the role of school counselor:	
Example: School counselors should deal with bullying situations	
What responsibilities and duties should the school counselor have?	**How much time should they spend on it?** *Include percentages if appropriate*
Example: Work on student schedules	*Example: The first two weeks of school*

This exercise can be used as a starting point to frame the conversation in the "Collaborative Data Reflection Activity" in the next section.

In *The ASCA National Model: A Framework for School Counseling Programs*, ASCA states,

> "the history of school counseling has been fraught with many twists and turns, leaving a trail littered with artifacts of each change of direction. As a result, the role of the school counselors and school counseling had not been clearly understood among school staff, administrators, families and even among school counselors themselves."[4]

Helping school leadership understand the distinction between the titles of guidance counselor, school counselor, or some combination is part of the role of a school counselor. The school counselor can help school leaders reflect on what is currently in place and how to best utilize school counselors to their fullest potential.

Put simply, the term guidance counselor harkens back to a time when the role was almost exclusively vocational in nature. Using the terms school counselor or professional school counselor exemplifies the more complex role the position holds and the expanded areas of student support that are provided. While the school counselor still provides vocational or career counseling, the new role requires master's-level training, practicum, and an internship to address the additional domains of social-emotional, mental health, and academics. For middle school counselors, understanding the unique developmental needs of young adolescents also shapes their role and interactions with students. In no uncertain terms, **middle school counselors effectively help students "construct the attitudes, values, and dispositions that will form who they become as adults."**[5]

In this new role, school counselors are vital to the whole school community. It is therefore critical that the CSCP is accessible and meaningful to all students. The school counselor can ensure this is the case by regularly checking for alignment with the ASCA National Model and The 18 Characteristics of Successful Middle Schools.

Through this alignment, the school counselor can provide all students the appropriate level of support and intervention in an intentional, data-backed manner. Their role becomes proactive rather than reactive. And when a school counselor aligns their CSCP with both the ASCA National Model and *The Successful Middle School*, they provide a more consistent level of support and intervention to all students than if only aligning their program to individual state standards. This will be covered in more detail in Section Two.

CHAPTER 3: THE ROLE OF SCHOOL ADMINISTRATORS

The Successful Middle School: This We Believe
Characteristics Crossover

- Leaders are committed to and knowledgeable about young adolescents, equitable practices, and educational research.
- Leaders demonstrate courage and collaboration.
- A shared vision developed by all stakeholders guides every decision.

Principals can support school counselors by giving them time, space, and resources to address the needs of students. Principals should ensure that counselors are not given duties outside of their recommended role that will take away time from providing direct and indirect services. It is crucial that school counselors are not put in the role of administrator as this alters the power balance between the school counselors and the students with whom they have forged trusting relationships. For example, it is not the role of school counselors to deal with a bullying issue that will become disciplinary. Probing for information can fracture the underlying trust of that relationship.

As the master scheduler, the principal should create protected time in the schedule for school counselors to facilitate counseling groups that don't detract from instructional time. As an instructional leader, the principal should support school counselors providing classroom guidance on a variety of topics that support students as well as promote collaboration on embedding social-emotional learning (SEL) competencies into daily instruction. Lastly, as a disciplinarian, the principal should ensure this role is not being delegated to school counselors. A better idea may be having the school counselor consult with the student throughout the discipline process to help them reflect on the situation and better understand the consequences involved. As the school head, the principal should collaborate consistently with the school counselor on ways to improve student success.

> **PRINCIPAL PERSPECTIVES**
>
> *As principal, have a vision for counselors to be able to provide comprehensive counseling and allowing for policies and practices to make it happen. Know how the counselors will fit into your strategic plan.*
>
> – Tyler Turner

From the school counselor perspective, the administrator should be a collaborator. Ideally, the principal and school counselor make time at the beginning of the year to review data from the previous year. Use what you already have available, including data on grades, attendance, test scores, discipline, and demographics. Reviewing data together sparks professional conversations about trends and needs, helping you target underserved groups. The school counselor and school principal can bring their respective knowledge and professional lenses to the conversation, providing a holistic approach that might not otherwise be visible. These conversations can change perspectives for the better and prevent misconceptions about each other's roles and duties. Complete the activity in Figure 1 to begin your collaborative data conversation (see Appendix A for reproducible version).

Figure 1 – Collaborative Data Reflection Activity

Discussion Topic	Suggested Data Points to Consider	Principal	School Counselor
Roles/Responsibilities: How does the counseling program or specific counselors fit into the school's strategic plan?	Goal data from the previous year		
Demographics: Do school policies and practices meet the needs of all students?	Enrollment data Special populations Course enrollment Intervention data		
Academic Achievement Data: How can the school counselor support this and at what tier?	Grades Assessments		
Discipline Data: How do school trends match data from the counseling program?	Perception data Needs assessment SEL surveys		
Attendance Data: How can services and interventions from school counseling assist in this area?	Tardies Absences Extreme cases of truancy Transiency data		

ASCA also offers an Annual Administrative Conference organizational template (Appendix B) to map your CSCP for the school year. Having an annual agreement completed within the first month of school increases the principal's knowledge of the school counselor's skills and how they align to other efforts to create a positive school climate and promote student achievement. Typically, the school counseling department completes a draft agreement and presents it to the principal for input and recommendations. This collaborative discussion ensures that the CSCP aligns with the vision and mission of the school and administrative goals. By taking time to intentionally plan and build strong lines of communication and collaboration, "the school counseling objectives and school-wide goals are so intertwined that it is almost impossible to tease them apart from each other."[6]

CHAPTER 4: THE ROLE OF TEACHERS

The Successful Middle School: This We Believe
Characteristics Crossover

- Educators respect and value young adolescents.
- Every student's academic and personal development is guided by an adult advocate.
- Professional learning for all staff should be relevant, long term, and job embedded.

The teacher's role in support of the CSCP is twofold: to understand and to collaborate. While teachers are the first responders in the classroom and often take on school counseling activities, their support is much more than that when it comes to the CSCP. First, teachers must understand the role and specific skills of professional school counselors; there is often a big misunderstanding of what school counselors actually do. How do we address this? Simply put, teach them. We ask teachers to know many things and, in the correct circumstances, we provide them with professional training. The case of educating on the CSCP is very much the same. Once teachers know and understand the role of school counselors, they can then better utilize the program's resources. Consider this agenda for professional development:

Sample Agenda

- The role of school counselor
- How school counselors should spend their time
- How a Comprehensive School Counseling Program fits into MTSS
- Direct and indirect services available to teachers and students
- How professional school counselors can help in the classroom

The teacher's second role in supporting the CSCP is true collaboration. In Section Three, we will discuss strategies to support this, but first let's address mindset. Meta-analysis researcher John Hattie found that collective teacher efficacy has one of the highest effect sizes in schools today. Collective efficacy is the shared belief of the school staff in their ability to positively affect students.[7] A school staff that believes it can accomplish great things and make a positive impact likely will.[8,9] Pairing the unique training of teaching and school counseling can be powerful in truly addressing the needs of students. In education, we refer to the training, skills, and experiences of educators as their "toolbox": the combined toolbox of teaching and school counseling is the best of all worlds. This toolbox serves as the rail system's sensors. Their purpose is to detect issues so that they can be addressed to avoid train derailment. The sensors work together to keep the train on course, much like teachers and school counselors work together to keep students on track and moving forward. Teachers must fully embrace the collaboration with school counselors and understand that collectively their reach can be broader and more responsive.

Our Train Sensors
Teacher-Counselor Partnership

Perhaps you're familiar with this saying: "You can't Bloom before you Maslow." But let's consider it another way. Bloom's work offers three domains: cognitive, affective, and psychomotor, with cognitive and psychomotor being the most prevalent in educational training programs and information.[10] As teachers we are taught to "get them thinking" or "get them up and moving." Conversely, "activate their values and emotions" isn't as ubiquitous. But with recent increased attention on social-emotional learning (SEL) and mental health, the affective domain has emerged as being of equal importance. Currently, 44 states require that SEL be implemented in schools through sheltered instruction of class lessons and activities or through daily classroom practices.[11] To learn more about state requirements, visit https://casel.org.

Teachers often ask, "Why is this initiative not being addressed by the school counselors?" We will go into more detail in Chapter 10 as to what SEL is and is not, as well as how the collaborative process between teachers and school counselors can enhance meeting both the identified competencies of SEL and school counseling standards at Tier 1. When we combine the best of teaching and school counseling practices, we can intentionally teach and reach all three of Bloom's domains and truly get to the center of student-centered learning.

CHAPTER 5: THE ROLE OF FAMILIES

The Successful Middle School: This We Believe
Characteristics Crossover

- The schools engage families as valued partners.

    "We need to relate to families not as clients, but as partners in school and community improvement."

    – Larry Ferlazzo

As young adolescents naturally start to push away from their parents and caregivers, this is the time we need families involved most. But how do we genuinely engage them as partners in their child's middle school journey? And more importantly, what role do families have in supporting the CSCP? Let's first talk about the varying levels of partnership between families and the school.

Inform

The informing level includes all the information schools send to families and the ways we send it, such as via websites, newsletters, school messaging systems, or social media. At this level, we are letting families know what is happening and how they can get involved. During the COVID-19 pandemic, information became more important than ever. Schools relied on families to read multiple communications; unfortunately, parents and caregivers often became so overwhelmed with the amount of information that they stopped reading. This was an important reminder that families need a variety of communication types, and that we need to ask them their preferred method and language for that communication.

Involve

At this level, families are doing a variety of things both at the school and at home. Depending on availability, it may look like volunteering, being a part of the PTA, dropping off items for school events, chaperoning a field trip, or being a guest speaker. We like to think of this level as time, talents, or treasures. Getting families involved at school provides them with a view into the lives of their children and the daily operations of the school. Both sides benefit from involvement.

Engage

Engaging families can mean different things in different contexts. Family engagement specialists from the Ohio Statewide Family Engagement Center assert that:

> "genuine family engagement is more than a well-attended open house or small booster group that raises funds for the school. Family engagement initiatives proven to be effective are balanced, equitable, reciprocal, and open partnerships that allow educators and families to share expertise and seek feedback in a mutually trusting way. Each role contributes to the shared goal of student success."[12]

When we consider this definition, engaging focuses efforts on the students and not simply getting families into the building. Engagement can be teaching families how to use the learning management system, enabling them to sit with their student and say "show me your work" or "show me what assignments you need to work on." Truly engaging families makes them a partner and gives them a say. Additional ideas to engage families are to:

- Create a School Counseling Program Advisory Council, which allows families to be an essential component of the CSCP. Not only do they lend their unique perspective on student needs, they become strong advocates for the program and can help communicate the program's services to the broader community. Host family information nights that families and students attend together.
- Hold parent and caregiver focus groups, reporting back to show how they were part of the decision-making process.
- Host a Meet the Teacher Night that isn't focused on agendas, syllabi, or anything related to instruction. Instead, use the time to get to know each other.
- In addition to the advisory council, create seats for parents and caregivers on school committees.
- Ask parents and caregivers to be a part of staff hiring committees.

Empower

We include empower as a level of partnership in part due to shifts we're seeing in society and schools. To empower is to grant someone power or authority by legal or official means. While that may sound counterintuitive to a partnership model, the reality is that schools are increasingly encountering families with strong demands about what education should look like for their child. We would not expect that by going for your annual physical your whole life that you would call yourself a doctor. However, what if for a year, maybe longer, you had to observe the doctor as they provided care? Might you have a broader perspective of and appreciation for their role? Families' windows into the world of education expanded during the COVID-19 pandemic, creating a shift in their perspective on what schooling should look like for their children. The key is to find mutual ground around the needs of the student and to keep that as the focus. It is in this scenario where we would say "lead with your ear."

It is here that when the school counseling department shines in helping families understand their role and how to best support their child. In our experience, we must teach families what the CSCP offers and how to access their school counselors. Schools can inform, involve, and engage families, empowering them with resources and support to make better decisions for their child. The school counseling department can listen and decipher needs to create a collaborative relationship. In turn, when we educate parents and caregivers on how to do this, the process is much easier. Through this collaborative and empowering process, school counselors can help advocate for students by understanding the families' expectations and needs.

Scenario – Lead with your ear. What would you do?

Your school counselor has set up a "Parent and Caregiver Coffee" as an information session for families on how they can help support their middle school student in study skills and organization. To ensure the event is as responsive as possible to its attendees, the school counselor distributes a survey to gauge comfort level and solicit feedback on specific areas the attendees want to address. The feedback was mixed. Some responses identified typical concerns such as motivating kids, or how to create buy-in. But there were other, unexpected responses. A surprising number of parents wondered why they should even need to attend the session, suggesting that the school must be "pawning off" the responsibility of study skills and organization on families.

Provide your answers below and then compare for alignment.

Principal Answer	School Counselor Answer

The Who: "The Train Depot"

CHAPTER 6: THE ROLE OF COMMUNITY

The Successful Middle School: This We Believe
Characteristics Crossover

- The school collaborates with community and business partners.
- Organizational structures foster purposeful learning and meaningful relationships.

We often say it takes a village to raise a child, but how often do we really put this into practice or view the general community as part of the whole-child stakeholder group? In schools, there are several ways to engage our community; the key, however, is making sure it is authentic and meaningful. The community can be one of the greatest assets for the CSCP in that they bring into the school outside expertise, additional perspectives, resources, and investment. But we must invite the community to be a part of the process. Once we establish relationships, there are many strategies we can use to continue to partner with our community.

Outside Expertise and Perspectives

Both the 18 Characteristics and the ASCA National Model highlight the need to develop college and career readiness for students. You can easily engage your community to help prepare students in these areas. This might include creating a guest speakers bureau that visits classrooms regularly or assists students in learning more about careers. Or you could host career fairs where community experts speak to students about local career opportunities.

Your community can also provide insight into what's happening in the local neighborhood. You might host school counseling coffees or chats that include members of the community to learn about outside happenings or discuss school-wide initiatives. It is enriching to hear other perspectives, especially from those outside of the school setting.

Resources and Investment

Community and business partners are well known for supporting schools both financially and with time. The entire community benefits when students have what they need to be successful. Here are a few examples of how these partnerships can support your CSCP:

- Create after-school opportunities for community partners to tutor students. Many companies incentivize or even require volunteer hours for their employees.
- Start a mentoring program, pairing community members with students.
- Start a food pantry at your school for students/families experiencing food insecurity and encourage community donations. You might then send that food home with students over the weekend.
- Create a fund that community members can donate to. Use the funds to purchase material needs or to provide temporary housing for displaced students.
- Have community partners sponsor school activities that are related to initiatives like *Positive Behavioral Interventions and Supports (PBIS)* or academic honors.

The possibilities are endless!

CHAPTER 7: THE ROLE OF STUDENT VOICE

The Successful Middle School: This We Believe
Characteristics Crossover

- Educators respect and value young adolescents.
- Every student's academic and personal development is guided by an adult advocate.
- The school environment is welcoming, inclusive, and affirming for all.

Picture this (and you may only need to go as far as a recent memory to do so): You are in a meeting with several stakeholders concerned about a student. This may include parents, teachers, school support personnel, and others. The adults are drawing from their observations, relationships, and data regarding the student to talk about how to support the student's success. Now picture the same discussion, but this time the student is in the room. How does that change the conversation? The student's presence in the meeting is powerful. Student voice has this same level of impact when implementing a CSCP.

Inviting student voice, as a strategy, is one of the most powerful things that schools can do for young adolescents. When we truly engage students and provide them with a seat at the table, there is more engagement, buy-in, and (more than likely) some strong opinions. Surveying more than 56,000 students, teachers, and parents, Quaglia and Corso found that student voice is one of the key ingredients missing from most school reform efforts.[13] They assert that it is not enough just to ask questions; we must listen as well. Their findings show that "when students believe their voices matter, they are more likely to be invested and engaged in their schools."[14] Students who are part of the process offer valuable feedback that helps schools meet their needs. When we think about feedback, we must remember that it is not one directional. While adult-to-student communication is important, so too is student-to-adult communication as it provides the groundwork for how to engage with students and identify what is important to them. Therefore, to truly engage student voice we must create schools that are psychologically safe and provide the circumstances for students to engage in discourse where the feedback is both heard and valued by adults.[15] Here are a few ways to engage student voice and solicit feedback to improve your schools.

Needs Assessment is a way to collect perception data from students and/or families at the beginning of the school year to identify student needs and plan for potential interventions. The plan should also include the tier in which the service would be implemented (see **Appendix C** for a sample needs assessments).

Advisory Council "is a representative group of stakeholders selected to review and advise on the implementation of the school counseling program."[16] Student representation is included as a stakeholder group, providing a forum for students to receive a clearer understanding of what school counselors are doing and to lend feedback on the effectiveness of the program.

Student Ambassador Program is a great way for students to involve themselves in the school community. Student ambassadors represent their school positively and help build community within the school through activities they help plan. Some ideas are to provide support to students and families who are new to the school, attend school events to support attendees in finding their way around the school, or provide feedback to leadership on ways the school could improve its culture.

Peer Mediators are a uniquely trained group of students who help their peers navigate difficult conversations where conflict is present. Peer mediation provides an opportunity for student leadership in your school community, as well as peer modeling of conflict resolution.

Volunteers for Transition Activities are those who offer insight and support to new students, easing the worry or anxiety that is sometimes associated with the unknown of a new school. Another option is to have students participate in a panel discussion where they answer questions from the new students. This is an empowering opportunity for young adolescents and their advice is well received by those who are beginning the middle school journey.

SECTION ONE REVIEW

Let's review the highlights of Section One. If you have completed the components suggested in Section One, your train's sensors are now active as you will have successfully:

1. Discussed assumptions vs. reality of school counselor roles and responsibilities;
2. Completed the collaborative data conversation with your school counselor;
3. Considered and developed professional learning for teachers around the roles and responsibilities of the school counselors/school counseling program;
4. Brainstormed new ways to engage families and/or created a School Counseling Program Advisory Council;
5. Considered new ways to involve your larger community and business partners; and

The Who: "The Train Depot"

6. Created a needs assessment or other way to engage student voice in your program.

To end Section One and begin Section Two, consider these reflection questions on how you will integrate the CSCP into the fabric of everything you do in the school.

Additional Questions for Reflection

- What assumptions have been challenged in this section as you reflect on how different stakeholders in your school play a role in the success of the school counseling program?
- What is a practice you might change moving forward to support the success of the school counseling program in your school?
- Which role were you the least familiar with as it pertains to the school counseling program?
- What resources or documents do you currently use to guide your Comprehensive School Counseling Program and evaluate its effectiveness?

Section Two
The What

Section Two

The What
"The Middle School Transportation System"

FOUNDATIONAL DOCUMENTS AND FRAMEWORKS FOR COMPREHENSIVE SERVICES

In Section One, we explored the "who" of the train depot—that is, the various roles and how each one can support the CSCP at your school. In this section, we will explore the "what." We will focus on foundational documents and frameworks that can shape your school's CSCP and how utilizing all of them can help you best meet the needs of young adolescents.

First, imagine yourself standing at a railroad crossing looking left to see what you know are vast miles of train tracks. Notice the rails. Their function is to keep the train on the tracks. But there isn't just one rail; there are two. Between those tracks are the ties, which have the main job of securing the rails and ensuring they stay upright and spaced correctly—helping to avoid a train wreck. Now look right. Here comes the engine built to power the train and tasked with safety and delivery. Remember, however, that the engine can't run without its crew and it won't make it to its destination without the rails and ties.

To begin this section, we will explore the 5 Essential Attributes and 18 Characteristics of *The Successful Middle School: This We Believe* alongside the ASCA National Model, each serving as a rail for your intricate transportation system known as middle school. We will then look at the CASEL Framework for social-emotional learning, which serves as the ties. Lastly, we will move our train with the engine: multi-tiered systems of support (MTSS). Let's get movin'!

CHAPTER 8: RAIL 1: THE 5 ESSENTIAL ATTRIBUTES AND THE 18 CHARACTERISTICS

The Successful Middle School: This We Believe
Characteristics Crossover

- Comprehensive counseling and support services meet the needs of young adolescents.

To begin building the first rail of our system, let's explore the 5 Essential Attributes and 18 Characteristics of *The Successful Middle School: This We Believe*. The Essential Attributes represent the essence of what we want and need in our schools to meet the needs of young adolescents. In its strategic plan, AMLE as its core value declares "unequivocally that ALL young adolescents deserve an education that is responsive, challenging, empowering, equitable, and engaging."[1] In the plan, these 5 Essential Attributes are defined as follows:

- **Responsive**: Using the distinctive nature and identities of young adolescents as the foundation upon which all decisions about school are made.

The Successful Middle School: This We Believe

Essential Attributes

AMLE affirms that an education for young adolescents must be:

Responsive
Using the distinctive nature and identities of young adolescents as the foundation upon which all decisions about school are made.

Challenging
Cultivating high expectations and advancing learning for every member of the school community.

Empowering
Facilitating environments in which students take responsibility for their own learning and contribute positively to the world around them.

Equitable
Providing socially just learning opportunities and environments for every student.

Engaging
Fostering a learning atmosphere that is relevant, participatory, and motivating for all learners.

Characteristics

Successful middle schools exhibit the following 18 characteristics:

Culture and Community

— Educators respect and value young adolescents.
— The school environment is welcoming, inclusive, and affirming for all.
— Every student's academic and personal development is guided by an adult advocate.
— School safety is addressed proactively, justly, and thoughtfully.
— Comprehensive counseling and support services meet the needs of young adolescents.
— The school engages families as valued partners.
— The school collaborates with community and business partners.

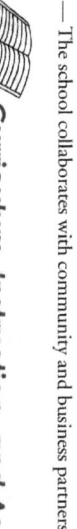

Curriculum, Instruction, and Assessment

— Educators are specifically prepared to teach young adolescents and possess a depth of understanding in the content areas they teach.
— Curriculum is challenging, exploratory, integrative, and diverse.
— Health, wellness, and social-emotional competence are supported in curricula, school-wide programs, and related policies.
— Instruction fosters learning that is active, purposeful, and democratic.
— Varied and ongoing assessments advance learning as well as measure it.

Leadership and Organization

— A shared vision developed by all stakeholders guides every decision.
— Policies and practices are student-centered, unbiased, and fairly implemented.
— Leaders are committed to and knowledgeable about young adolescents, equitable practices, and educational research.
— Leaders demonstrate courage and collaboration.
— Professional learning for all staff is relevant, long term, and job embedded.
— Organizational structures foster purposeful learning and meaningful relationships.

From **the Successful Middle School: This We Believe**, published by the Association for Middle Level Education. Build your own professional development plan with the Successful Middle School program.

Visit **amle.org/sms**

- **Challenging**: Cultivating high expectations and advancing learning for every member of the school community.
- **Empowering**: Facilitating environments in which students take responsibility for their own learning and contribute positively to the world around them.
- **Equitable**: Providing socially just learning opportunities and environments for every student.
- **Engaging**: Fostering a learning atmosphere that is relevant, participatory, and motivating for all learners.

One of the most important aspects of school leadership is fostering a positive school culture that is inviting, inclusive, and safe. As the saying goes, "Culture trumps strategy, every time."[2] Further, cultivating an environment where everyone understands young adolescents and their needs makes it a place where everyone can grow. School culture shapes the daily behavior of faculty and students and must be treated with the utmost care and attention. Carefully reflecting on how the CSCP fits into that equation is equally important. As we continue to build our rail system, take a few minutes to reflect on the Essential Attributes and how well your organization embraces them. This may be your starting point for this ride.

> **PRINCIPAL PERSPECTIVES**
>
> I wish I had known the unspoken work they do to help staff. I've witnessed our counselors helping staff deal with the emotional aspects of their jobs—when they feel overwhelmed, inept, frustrated, etc.
>
> – Dru Tomlin

The What: "The Middle School Transportation System"

Research tells us that these core values are realized through 18 Characteristics of Successful Middle Schools, the first rail of our tracks. These Characteristics are grouped by three overarching categories: Culture and Community; Curriculum, Instruction, and Assessment; Leadership and Organization. Embedded throughout this book are connections to the 18 Characteristics to help schools explore how they apply in the larger context of the CSCP. You can read more about the 18 Characteristics in *The Successful Middle School: This We Believe*. For our purposes, we will provide a brief summary of the overarching categories and how they apply to the CSCP.

Reflection Questions

- When you think about your current school culture, does it embrace these core values?
- Does your current counseling program facilitate these attributes through its programming and daily interactions with teachers, students, and families?

Jot down some ideas of how you could embrace these attributes as your own core values and make them a part of your school culture.

Culture and Community

The Characteristics within this category encompass culture in terms of respect, environment, advocacy, and safety; not just physical safety, but psychological safety as well. Schools are encouraged to partner with families while engaging the larger community to round out the middle school experience. Middle schools who have focused on culture and community attend to the overall experience of young adolescents to ensure that it is affirming and designed specifically to meet their needs academically, socially and emotionally, and physically. These Characteristics help schools foster the joy of learning and develop the whole child.

> **PRINCIPAL PERSPECTIVES**
>
> *Communication both in and out of the counseling office is vital to the success of the school.*
>
> – Nino Collado

We must think both globally and granularly when we think about the comprehensive school counseling department and the role it plays in school culture. As you aligned your thinking and planning in Section One, you were able to see the vital role of the CSCP in crafting a positive culture and sense of community. When we think globally, the CSCP serves all students in the school. It helps set the tone for student advocacy and interactions with students, staff, families, and the greater community.

The What: "The Middle School Transportation System"

Alongside the administration, the program invites students and families into the building and is often the first exposure students and families have to the school.

When we think granularly about the CSCP, the reach is vast. School counselors interface daily with both staff and students. In addition to their other duties, their time is spent doing both direct and indirect service. In our own experience, school counselors help model interactions with students and families, and are tasked with ensuring the communication is transparent and multi-directional. As advocates, school counselors tease out the needs of students and work collaboratively with staff and families to meet them. School counselors, essentially, help to put all the pieces together to lay a foundation for culture and community.

Lastly, school counselors should have a high visibility both in and out of the classroom as they assist students and collaborate with teachers. It is in this way that school counselors do much more than work with students. More prevalent now than in years past, the role of school counselor has expanded to include assisting or supporting teachers as they navigate difficult situations, including responding to behavioral, academic, or social-emotional concerns in the classroom. As part of indirect services, the school counselor acts in a consultative role to assist the teacher in planning and responding to the needs of students. As the needs of schools continue to evolve, so too will this aspect of the CSCP.

> **COUNSELOR CALL IN**
>
> *Lots of teachers don't like us pulling kids out of class because they don't believe there is a need. This is stressful for us and cuts down on the time we have to work with students. There needs to be collaboration.*
>
> —Lindsay Carr

Culture and Community Activity

Below, list key aspects of your school culture and the role school counselors play; include both direct and indirect services. If school counselors are currently not part of your culture, think about changes you can make to ensure that they are.

Key Aspect of Culture	Counselor Role	Direct, Indirect, or Both
Example: Student voice is valued	Example: Working with administration to solicit student voice and act on it	Indirect: Working with administration Direct: Working directly with students on issues they deem important

Curriculum, Instruction, and Assessment

The Characteristics within this area address quality instruction and everything it takes to meet the needs of young adolescents in the classroom. It is not just about standards, but how we prepare teachers to understand and reach young adolescents while making classrooms engaging, inviting, and challenging. Instruction for middle school students focuses on depth of thinking and understanding while capturing their needs to develop social-emotional skills as well as their own identities. As varied as the students in our classrooms, educators should assess in the same way while using the data to inform instruction and plan for active, purposeful learning.

The What: "The Middle School Transportation System"

Curriculum	Instruction	Assessment

Curriculum for school counselors is:
• Guided by state and national standards and competencies and/or ASCA Mindsets and Behaviors
• Guided by standards for health and wellness of students
• Collaboratively developed and delivered with classroom teachers to ensure that SEL competencies are not seen as something different, but something that is taught in conjunction with content standards
	School counselors provide instruction in a variety of ways and settings, including:
	
	• Working individually with students
	• Conducting small groups for specific needs
	• Classroom lessons
	  ○ Academic planning
	  ○ Career exploration
	  ○ Healthy relationships
	• Collaboratively delivering lessons with teachers
	• Parent and caregiver workshops
	• Staff professional development
		School counselors administer a variety of assessments to determine needs and effectiveness of school counseling services and interventions. Some examples include:
		
		• Beginning-of-year needs assessment
		• Ongoing monitoring of student achievement and interventions for goal setting
		• Student completion surveys to assess value of services or groups that have been delivered
		• Number of students who receive instruction in a variety of areas

While only specifically mentioned in Culture and Community, programming and services from the CSCP are also applicable to Curriculum, Instruction, and Assessment. Below are a few of the ways that these Characteristics apply to how school counselors serve students.

Regardless of the setting, school counselors work to ensure that their instruction is developmentally appropriate and centered on student needs. Their intended audience helps guide both the content and context for the instruction. In consultation, school counselors can assist classroom teachers with teasing out issues when students have difficulty managing classroom expectations for achievement and behavior, or if environmental factors are impeding learning (more on this in Chapter 11). The ongoing assessments that school counselors conduct, and the feedback they receive from teachers and students, helps them to know if services are working and guides the next steps in their process. The data gathered from these assessments helps school counselors determine trends in students' perception of their own personal needs which can help with programming, groups, or classroom lessons.

Inventory Check
Consider additional strategies that your counseling program uses for curriculum, instruction, and assessment and list them below.

Strategy	Curriculum, Instruction, or Assessment?
Example: Universal screener for social-emotional learning (SEL)	*Example: Assessment*

The What: "The Middle School Transportation System"

Leadership and Organization

The Characteristics within this area address how, guided by a shared vision, we lead and organize our middle schools to best meet the needs of young adolescents. Leaders must ensure that school policies and practices are student centered, unbiased, and fairly implemented. Being unbiased requires leaders to understand that regardless of their beliefs, they will still see every situation through their own lens of experience and must make sure that lens does not cloud their judgment about students, staff, or families. Staying current on research and best practices for meeting the needs of young adolescents is modeled by leadership and embedded in ongoing professional learning for staff. It is within this area we embrace the true meaning of collective responsibility and shared leadership.

> **PRINCIPAL PERSPECTIVES**
>
> *One big lesson I learned is that what we actually have counselors do is not what they are trained to do. Working directly with school counselors and leadership teams can help build a schedule where counselors are able to work with small groups, handle initial intakes for mental health needs, and help students prepare for college and career. In my experience, we often used them as academic guidance counselors and missed the boat on the SEL support they are trained to provide due to a systems error.*
>
> – Majalise Tolan

In Section One, we asked you to think about the role of the CSCP and where it fits into your strategic plan. When we collectively develop our vision, which should guide all our decisions, this seems like it would be an easy task. However, due to lack of knowledge about the function or potential of CSCPs, school counseling is often siloed. School counselors are either handed the school improvement plan and asked to add strategies, or spend their time trying to fit the square peg into the round hole. In some cases, school counselors, either by a deficit in alignment or misunderstanding of the role, are seen as a separate entity that "sees students who are in crisis" or "are responsible for the advisory program." When we have a shared vision, we include the CSCP as part of daily operations. School counseling programs are, by nature, designed to be student centered and focus on advocacy; therefore, as leaders, we must ensure that counseling is a part of our policies, practices, and everyday business operations.

CHAPTER 9: THE ASCA NATIONAL MODEL: RAIL 2

The Successful Middle School: This We Believe
Characteristics Crossover

- Comprehensive counseling and support services meet the needs of young adolescents.
- Every student's academic and personal development is guided by an adult advocate.
- Health, wellness, and social-emotional competence are supported in curricula, school-wide programs, and related policies.

The American School Counselor Association (ASCA) serves as the professional organization specifically designed to meet the needs of school counselors. With permission, we are using the ASCA National Model to highlight its importance in developing a Comprehensive School Counseling Program designed to meet the needs of young adolescents. Learn more about ASCA at schoolcounselor.org.

ASCA encourages school counselors to meet the needs of all students by aligning their CSCP with the ASCA National Model. Originally introduced in 2003

The What: "The Middle School Transportation System"

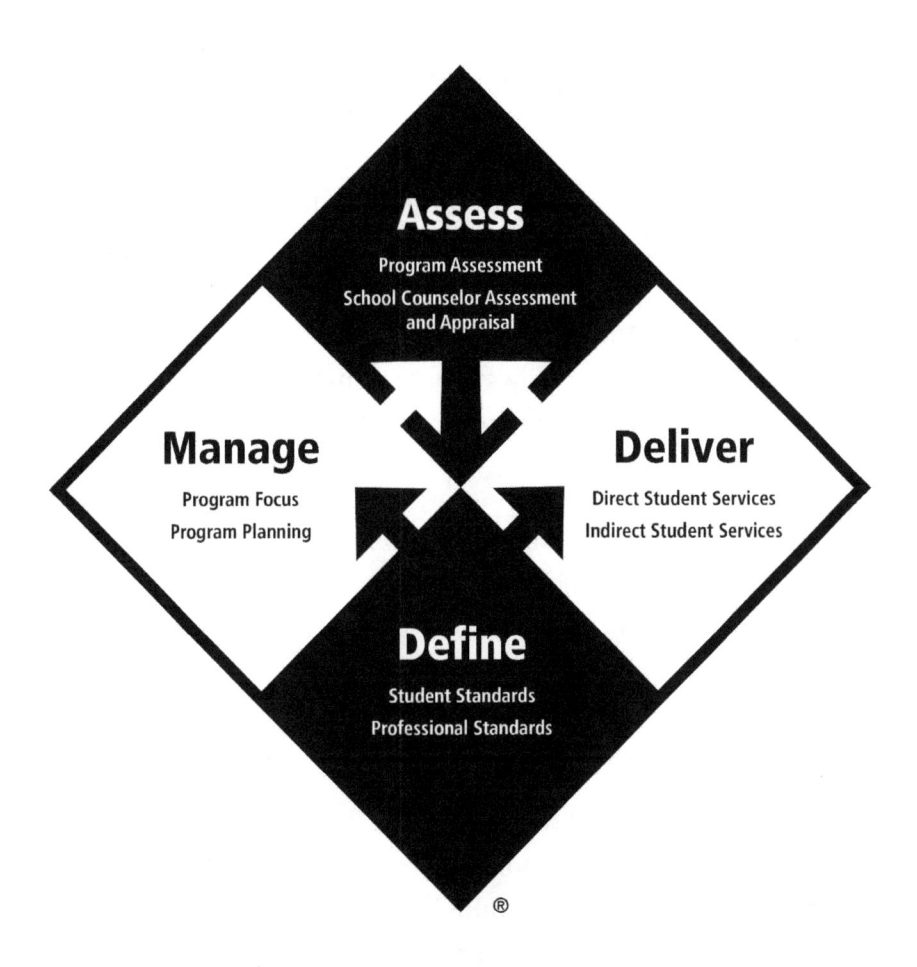

Assess
Program Assessment
School Counselor Assessment and Appraisal

Manage
Program Focus
Program Planning

Deliver
Direct Student Services
Indirect Student Services

Define
Student Standards
Professional Standards

and currently under the 2019 edition, the ASCA framework provides guidance to support Comprehensive School Counseling Programs to ensure that the work and services they provide are truly meeting the needs of all students in an intentional and ethical way. The ASCA National Model is divided into four components: Define, Manage, Deliver, and Assess, and helps the program organize, implement, manage, and assess needs and program effectiveness.[3] As you can see from the visual representation of the ASCA National Model, the components do not represent the typical cyclical process. They are grounded in the foundational **DEFINE** component which feeds into the **MANAGE** and **DELIVER** components. These two components directly inform the **ASSESS** component. Much like the perspective exercise of seeing either a duck or a rabbit in the picture, you can see that the arrows from the manage and deliver components create an arrow from assess back to define.

In this chapter, we will explore each component in terms of the elements it shares with other practices in highly effective middle schools. As those different shared practices are highlighted, we challenge you to reflect on how collaboration can occur with all stakeholders to ensure that student needs are being met effectively and efficiently. When a CSCP aligns itself to the ASCA National Model, it provides the second rail in our railway system that runs alongside the Essential Attributes and Characteristics of *The Successful Middle School: This We Believe*.

Expert Advice: ASCA recommends a ratio of 250:1 of students to school counselors to have a positive impact on student growth. Take time to review your state and/or district planning factors to see if there is alignment with this recommendation.

DEFINE

The ASCA National Model is driven by professional, ethical, and student standards that help to define the program and how it will serve students. The professional standards require that school counselors possess a set of skills, knowledge, and attitudes that help both students and school counselors to grow academically or professionally. Whether your school has a school counseling director, coordinator, lead school counselor, or maybe none of those, it is important to familiarize yourself with the standards as they provide the foundation for development and implementation of the comprehensive counseling program.

The ASCA Student Standards: Mindsets and Behaviors for Student Success are based on a meta-analysis of research and best practices for achievement gathered from a variety of standards and efforts. The ASCA Student Standards include "mindsets and behaviors for student success that describe the knowledge, attitudes and skills students need to achieve academic success, college and career readiness, and social/emotional development."[4] School counselors

The What: "The Middle School Transportation System"

use a variety of data sources in conjunction with reviewing the standards in order to "define" what the services will look like organized by the domains: academic, career, and social-emotional. This process includes creating goals for the year and collaborating with administration on a shared vision and mission that is aligned with the school improvement plan. Through defining the program, school counselors can demonstrate how their efforts are an essential part of the school initiatives and priorities.[5]

The DEFINE component starts with one of the most significant ways that the school counseling program and administration should collaborate: creating the CSCP's own vision and mission in alignment with the building's vision and mission. This is where the CSCP ensures that their "why" is aligned with the school building and district's "why." This process ensures that the school counseling program is not siloed and the shared "vision lights the way toward achieving a responsive and equitable education for every young adolescent."[6]

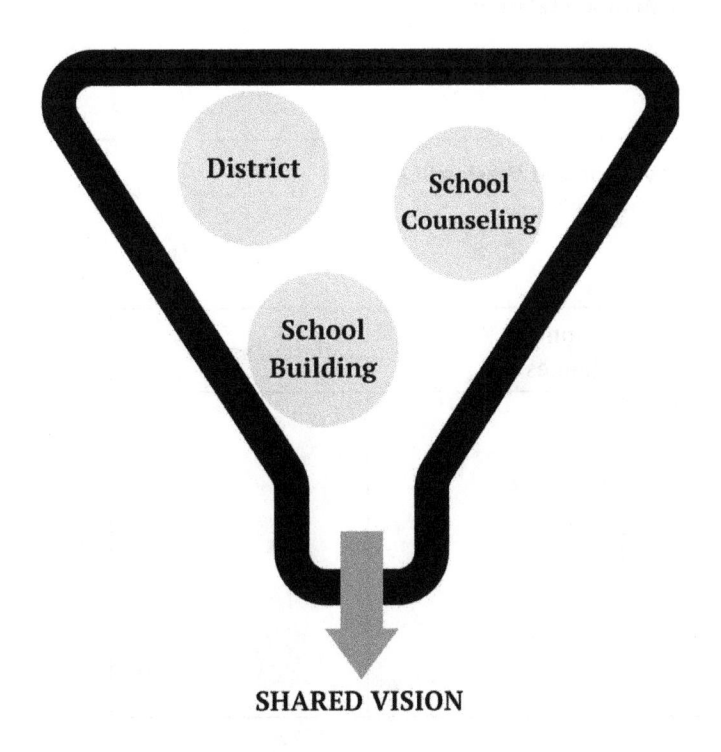

SHARED VISION

Reflection Activity: Evaluating the Shared Vision and Mission

Does your CSCP have a vision and mission of their own?
If not, here are three quick steps to develop one:

1. Each member of the department creates individual belief statements.
2. The whole department then compares and establishes common beliefs.
3. The department reaches consensus to then draft the vision and mission statements.

Locate your school and counseling program vision and mission statements and place them in the boxes below. Evaluate the text to find common language, themes, differences, and additional areas you may want to include in your counseling vision/mission.

School Vision and Mission Statement *Vision*: *Mission*:			
School Counseling Visions and Mission Statement *Vision*: *Mission*:			
Common Language	Common Themes	Differences	Areas to Change or Include

The What: "The Middle School Transportation System"

Example

School Vision and Mission Statement
Vision: Empowering all students to be lifelong learners and responsible citizens.
Mission: We are an inclusive school community committed to academic excellence and integrity. We recognize the needs of young adolescents to be empowered and have a voice in their learning; therefore, we will provide instruction in a caring, safe, and healthy environment responsive to each student in collaboration with families and community.

School Counseling Visions and Mission Statement
Vision: Develop the knowledge and skills students need to be successful lifelong learners and globally-minded citizens capable of achieving their goals.
Mission: Help promote equity, access, and high levels of learning for all students. We provide all students with a welcoming, comprehensive program that facilitates academic and personal success and college and career readiness through individual and group counseling, classroom lessons and school-wide activities. We foster appropriate student self-advocacy skills and integrity; promote partnerships among students, families, and staff; and empower students to be responsible members of our community.

Common Language	Common Themes	Differences	Areas to Change or Include
Lifelong learners	*Inclusivity*	*Promote equity*	*Include student voice*

Much like classroom teachers look to state or district standards to map the school year for student learning, CSCPs use the ASCA Mindsets and Behaviors to support student growth in categories of academic, career, and social-emotional domains. Note that the ASCA Student Standards are at the competency level.[7] Programs located in non-Common Core states are encouraged to align competencies with their own state counseling standards. If you have not done so, we suggest looking at your state's school counseling requirements to help support your school counseling program. There are opportunities in this component to analyze where the school counseling program standards intersect with other standards such as SEL or health and physical education. We will explore embedding standards more in Section Three.

In Section One, you completed the collaborative data activity to determine how the school counseling program would be included in your school plan. In the DEFINE component, school leadership and the school counseling department should combine their practices to develop data-driven goals for student improvement. Focus areas could include the whole child, social-emotional, attendance, and discipline.

> *Reflection Questions*
> - Do you include your school counseling department or school counseling leadership in your annual school plan goals?
> - If not, think of how you would and include your notes below. Consider the goals of the whole child, social-emotional learning, attendance, or discipline.

MANAGE

The MANAGE component is arguably the most identifiable area where school administrators and teachers can connect their own practices to the CSCP. The practices in this component are easily correlated to many best practices for the beginning of a school year and those found in MTSS. This component involves analysis of school data to identify areas of growth, student concern, or closing of gaps which informs services and interventions that contribute to and support student learning.

The What: "The Middle School Transportation System"

If your CSCP is at the beginning stages of ASCA National Model alignment, or has an area of growth in effective data analysis, this is an opportunity to have other instructional leaders or coaches in the building help them develop strength in analyzing data to identify needs. A proficient CSCP can effectively pull and analyze school data to identify areas where the program can further support student growth. In addition, the school counseling program can identify areas where additional data needs to be gathered, many times in the form of perception data such as AMLE's Successful Middle School Assessment[1]. This typically takes the form of needs assessments administered to students, families, and teachers. It can also be a survey from a third-party vendor in areas such as social-emotional competencies or career exploration. We propose that the unique perspective of data analysis of school counselors will result in creation of positive members of collaborative and interdisciplinary teams.

> **COUNSELOR CALL IN**
>
> *There are instructional areas of support building leadership can provide to support school counselors. Do any of your school counselors need additional professional development on collecting and/or analyzing outcome data?*
>
> —Anonymous

In our experience, we have not commonly seen school counselors specifically included as a part of regular operations of collaborative and interdisciplinary teams.

---

[1] For more information about the successful middle school assessment visit https://amle.org/SMS.

The Successful Middle School Counseling Program

It often looks like school counselors coming into meetings that are either for day-to-day operations discussions, "team meetings" that include student concerns, or possibly meetings about specific students. Rarely do school counselors attend content or team meetings to contribute to student growth in learning standards. However, as content teachers look at the data of a student who is underperforming in an area, the school counselor will have a unique perspective on that student and be able to troubleshoot other possible interventions besides content-based ones. The solution could include a combination of strategies. As an example, a student who needs grief counseling may be able to remain attentive in class when receiving an intervention because the needs are being met by the counselor.

MANAGE Activity

In the chart below, list ideas of common student content concerns and how the school counselor might support this concern.

Student Concern	Academic Intervention	School Counselor Intervention
Example: Deficit in reading	Example: MTSS period of day for instruction in specific reading strategies	Example: School counselor visits the MTSS reading intervention class weekly to work on stress management when reading becomes difficult

The What: "The Middle School Transportation System"

In Section One, you completed the perceptions vs. reality exercise where you reflected on your understanding and assumptions of the school counselor role. As mentioned in that chapter, not all school administrators have a robust understanding of the role of the CSCP. Knowing this, one can imagine how limited the family and community understanding of school counseling might be. Another essential area of the MANAGE component is the advisory council, which is "a representative group of stakeholders selected to review and advise on the implementation of the school counseling program."[8] As a result of the advisory council, a school counseling program receives input from a variety of stakeholders to help improve practices. More importantly, it creates a group that understands, advocates, and can communicate your CSCP's accomplishments.

Creating an Advisory Council

When identifying stakeholders to involve in the advisory council, it is important to have representation from both the school and community. Below are roles you might consider for membership:

- Some representative roles inside the school can include: teachers, students, and administration.
- Some representative roles from the community can include: parents, local community members, school board members, and even the owner of the favorite after-school local establishment of students.

The council should be well rounded and represent all facets of your school and community.

DELIVER

In this component, school counselors plan and evaluate where they are providing services to support student need. ASCA recommends that a minimum of 80% of school counselors' time be spent in either direct or indirect services delivery.[9] Direct service is any time that a school counselor is interacting directly with a student. This can be individual counseling, small group, classroom lessons, or large group instruction. Indirect time is not directly with students, but spent in activities that support the growth or improvement of student needs. Indirect services can include, but are not limited to, parent meetings, teacher consultation, and student support meetings. ASCA does not recommend non-school counselor roles, such as lunch duty, be included as part of school counselor time allocation. Rather, roles such as supervising a school counseling intern would be appropriate and encouraged for professional growth. Given these recommendations from ASCA, and understanding the many needs and staffing challenges in schools, it is understandable that schools may assign roles to school counselors that fall outside of those recommendations. Take a few minutes to complete the reflection activity below to inventory how your school counselors may be spending their time and consider possible modifications.

DELIVER Activity

List what roles or duties school counselors currently fill in your school. Then categorize them as direct service, indirect service, programming, or non-counselor activities. If much of the list is non-counselor activities, consider revising assignments.

Role or Duty	Type of Service	Alternatives
Example: School counselors review course grades and hold goal setting conferences with students	Direct service	None
Example: 504 case management	Non-counselor	Other staff with expertise in the disabling condition or specific staff to handle 504 case management

The What: "The Middle School Transportation System"

ASSESS

As a school leader, how do you ASSESS the success of the school's practices throughout the year? What comes to mind? Is it end-of-year state assessments, internal screeners, perception data, or all of the above? The end-of-year data review helps you evaluate how far your practices have moved students forward. A CSCP is no different. This assessment of student growth informs the impact the school counseling program had on students. ASCA acknowledges three major types of assessment to look at for program improvement: perception, outcome, and process.[10]

- **Perception data** is valuable to obtain stakeholder voice and get feedback on what knowledge was gained as a result of a school counselor intervention or activity. This data can be collected in the form of needs assessments or exit tickets at the end of a lesson or parent presentation.

- **Outcome data** is collected to help the CSCP demonstrate its effect on a common goal of school improvement.

- **Process data** highlights how many students are reached as a result of the CSCP or the success of a "process" implemented by the CSCP. This data is also valuable if the school needs to advocate for additional school counselors to provide support to students.

It is through careful thought, collaboration, and implementation that the ASCA National Model provides a holistic approach to comprehensive school counseling services. Ongoing evaluation of the program and consistent review of data helps the program be responsive to the students it serves. The process is ongoing and changes as the needs of teachers and students change, yet is always grounded in its definition and shared vision and mission.

CHAPTER 10: RAIL TIES: SOCIAL-EMOTIONAL LEARNING AND THE CASEL FRAMEWORK

The Successful Middle School: This We Believe
Characteristics Crossover

- Educators respect and value young adolescents.
- Every student's academic and personal development is guided by an adult advocate.

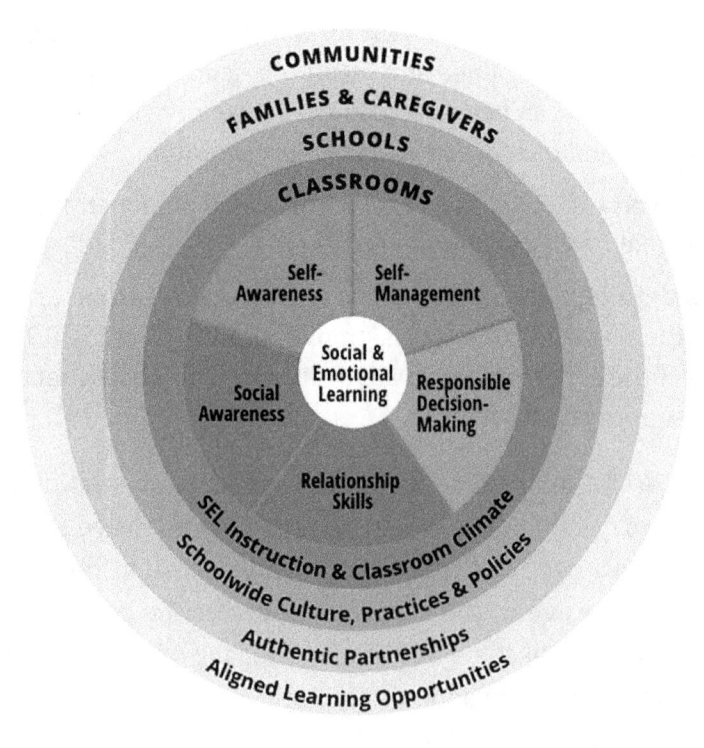

"The story of SEL is as old as the first relationships between teachers and students."

– CASEL

Before we begin this section, take a few minutes to reflect on your experience with and knowledge of SEL.

The What: "The Middle School Transportation System"

SEL Pre-Test Activity

What do you think of first when you hear the words social-emotional learning?	
What is your definition of SEL?	
What does SEL look like in practice?	
Who is responsible for SEL?	

We chose to include SEL as its own section for two reasons: 1. SEL is NOT just the work of school counselors; and 2. increased focus on social-emotional well-being and skills of students is absolutely necessary, especially given current trends in society and schools. As we work both in and with schools, we are frequently asked by non-counseling staff why they have to teach SEL lessons. Or are asked by school counselors why SEL is solely their responsibility. We hear statements like, "this is just something else we have to do." Most frequently, we hear that "we see the value, but how do we have the time to do this?" To answer questions like these, it is important to clarify the purpose of SEL, what it is, and how SEL must have shared goals between both instructional staff and the CSCP.

The increased focus on the regression of students' social-emotional skills over the past several years due to disrupted or virtual learning makes it important to understand what SEL is. This helps us to infuse the standards and competencies into day-to-day teacher and staff interactions with students. Given that most schools are already implementing some type of SEL, it is important to assess implementation and evaluate its effectiveness in the same way a school would approach any area of student academic growth (such as student literacy growth).

The Successful Middle School Counseling Program

The Successful Middle School: This We Believe references social-emotional competence throughout the text. This reinforces the foundational value of social-emotional learning for all aspects of student learning. Because of this, we see SEL competencies as the ties that hold the train rails together, providing a shared focus to ensure that these areas of student growth are always kept in mind throughout the middle school journey.

For this chapter, we have assumed the role of state, or national, academic standards to be a part of everyday instruction; therefore, we will focus on the SEL standards and how they help tie everything together.

Reflection Questions
- How is SEL currently being implemented at your school?
- Is SEL embedded throughout the day and infused into instruction?

Jot your reflections below.

Social-Emotional Learning Defined

The Collaborative for Academic, Social, and Emotional Learning (CASEL) defines SEL as "the process through which all young people and adults acquire and apply the knowledge, skills, and attitudes to develop healthy identities, manage emotions and achieve personal and collective goals, feel and show empathy for others, establish and maintain supportive relationships, and make responsible and caring decisions." The Committee for Children includes terms such as interpersonal skills, self-awareness, and self-control in their definition.[11] Positive Action adds ideas around helping people make informed choices and develop unique goals.[12] All of these organizations' definitions include wording around success in school and life. In our experience, we have heard SEL defined as the "soft skills" we teach. However, we challenge that perspective because the ability to build relationships, show empathy, set goals, and make sound decisions are not soft skills. Instead, they are essential, tangible skills necessary to navigate the middle school years. In fact, when we consider the developmental needs of young adolescents, some might say these are the most important skills.

John Hattie's newest research shows that teacher-student relationships maintain an optimal effect size of .62 in the classroom.[13] Conversely, students feeling disliked has an effect size of -.26. The combination of relationships, trust, competence, and enthusiasm, which make up teacher credibility, comes in at 1.09. SEL is not just "something else" we do; it is the essence of the way we do business. Researchers type this behavior as "intentionally inviting."[14] Teachers (and staff) who intentionally create an environment that is inviting and safe, and therefore conducive to relationships and learning, possess the following traits:

- Consistent and steady with students
- Notice learning and struggle
- Respond regularly with feedback
- Seek to build, maintain, and repair relationships

By clearly defining what SEL is and its importance across the school environment, we begin to shape the mantra that the work of embedding SEL is everyone's responsibility.[2]

---

[2] A note on Hattie's effect sizes: The effect sizes are created using meta-analysis with the hinge point of d=0.4 being the mean of all effect sizes. Those above 0.4 are considered to be in the zone of desired effects.

As you continue to work through the rest of this section, think of your own working definition of SEL. One of the best ways to do this is to work out "what it is" and "what it is not." In the boxes below, please write your statements:

SEL is ...	SEL is NOT...
Example: Helping students learn the skills of self-awareness	*Example: Teaching students your own personal values and beliefs*

CASEL Framework or "Wheel"

From 1987 to 1992, researchers Shriver and Weissberg, with colleagues, led the creation of the New Haven Social Development program that introduced the first set of SEL strategies for K–12 education. To further that work, Weissberg led a different group of educators and researchers through the WT Grant Consortium that was focused on school-based promotion of social competence. Through nearly a decade of work, the groups developed what they called the "missing" piece of education that addresses the social and emotional needs of children. It was in 1994 that the Collaborative for Academic, Social, and Emotional Learning (CASEL) and the term social-emotional learning were born.

CASEL is considered a leading, research-based organization for SEL. Its framework has either been adopted by states or serves as the foundational work guiding their policy, practices, and SEL initiatives. In *The Successful Middle School: This We Believe*, there is direct reference to the specific CASEL competencies in "curriculum that supports student health, wellness and social emotional competence." Additionally, it states that responsive middle grades schools offer "opportunities to develop skills and adopt mindsets that will help them succeed in life: self- and social-awareness,

The What: "The Middle School Transportation System"

self-management, relationship skills, and responsible decision-making." Also aligned with the CASEL framework are the ideas of students getting to know themselves, building relationships, setting goals, and becoming active members of the community.

The CASEL 5

CASEL has developed five areas of SEL competence designed to be taught developmentally.[3] These areas, with abbreviated definitions, are:

- Self-awareness: Develop a healthy sense of who we are
- Self-management: Manage stress and emotions to achieve goals
- Social-awareness: Understand the views of others, perspective taking, and empathy
- Relationship skills: Engage effectively with others, build relationships, communicate, and advocate
- Responsible decision making: Make caring and constructive choices

It is in the development of these competencies that we create inviting, safe, and equitable learning environments. Moreover, it is a systematic approach to SEL that leverages the power of bringing academic and social-emotional learning together. Every interaction with students should help them practice and refine their SEL competencies and further their learning. When we consider the needs of young adolescents, we must carefully design our instruction to include opportunities to grow their perspective of the world around them. Instruction should include deliberate experiences to build and repair relationships, practice interactions and advocacy, and learning strategies to manage emotions and stress. In other words, prepare them for the chance that their train might go off the rails.

In the spaces on the next page, brainstorm ways to reinforce these competencies for the students in your middle school. Consider the specific and developmental needs of young adolescents as you work. For additional assistance see the section on Young Adolescent Development and Implications for Educators in *The Successful Middle School: This We Believe*.

---

[3] See casel.org for additional information and resources

Competence Area	Strategies or Activities to Teach/Reinforce
Self-Awareness	
Self-Management	
Social-Awareness	
Relationship Skills	
Responsible Decision Making	

CASEL Key Settings

Surrounding the five competencies on the CASEL wheel are the Key Settings. This important part of the framework includes the context in which SEL is taught. It reinforces that connecting the "broader systems" that shape the learning and development of students results in a more holistic and systematic approach. The Key Settings and their focus include:

- **Classrooms:** SEL Instruction and Classroom Climate
  - Includes explicit instruction of skills
- **Schools**: School-Wide Culture, Practices, and Policies
  - Includes considering the overall experience of students in relation to discipline, relationships, and modeling by adults
- **Families and Caregivers**: Authentic Partnerships
  - Includes listening and partnering with families to support students
- **Communities**: Aligned Learning Opportunities
  - Includes aligning efforts to create opportunities outside of the school

The What: "The Middle School Transportation System"

The school counseling department can help bring this to life as the entity that is directly connected to all of these environments. Not only are they a part of daily operations in the school, but their time is also spent connecting with families and creating community partnerships to bring in resources or build career exploration connections. ASCA alignment ensures that counseling services meet the recommended Mindsets and Behavior Standards, included in CASEL research, which assists students in navigating all aspects of school and community life. This use of CASEL research makes the school counseling department ideal for collaborating, enhancing, and offering SEL implementation across all settings. The shared decision making and leadership between administration and counseling can help craft the vision for embedded SEL to ensure that it is a classroom-, school-, family-, and community-wide effort.

The Successful Middle School Counseling Program

Key Setting Quick Check

Rate your current systematic implementation across the Key Settings on a 1–5 scale, where 1 = "not yet" and 5 = "we do this consistently." When you are finished, reflect on areas of growth and possible goals you can set.

All staff teach SEL lessons	1	2	3	4	5
Explicitly teaching SEL competencies is embedded in regular classroom instruction	1	2	3	4	5
SEL is a part of our school-wide culture	1	2	3	4	5
Student voice is valued and acted upon	1	2	3	4	5
Student discipline is consistent	1	2	3	4	5
Student voice is included in the discipline process	1	2	3	4	5
Relationships are healthy and modeled for students	1	2	3	4	5
The overall experience of students is important	1	2	3	4	5
Families and caregivers are an integral part of our school	1	2	3	4	5
We listen and act on feedback from families and caregivers	1	2	3	4	5
We partner with our community to include students in outside activities	1	2	3	4	5
Students have opportunities to practice their competence in community activities	1	2	3	4	5

Areas of Growth

Possible Goals

The What: "The Middle School Transportation System"

As you can see, the role of SEL is much more than "something else" or "something we do in advisory." SEL is foundational to everyday interactions both in and out of school. While not their sole responsibility, the school counseling department is a key player. Given their specific training and expertise in students' expected social-emotional growth, the school counselor can help ensure a systematic approach that is developmentally appropriate to middle school. Additionally, school counselors have experience working with a variety of stakeholders, both in collaborative work to support students and in communicating the positive impact that social-emotional instruction and intervention has on student growth. Lastly, the school counseling department can assist in the deliberate planning and execution of SEL and how to measure its effectiveness. More detail on specific strategies will be included in Section Three.

> **SEL Post-Test**
>
> Review your answers to the pre-test. Has anything changed in your answers? What might you consider changing if the answer was yes?

Your Learning

Changes You Want to Make

CHAPTER 11: THE ENGINE: MULTI-TIERED SYSTEMS OF SUPPORT

The Successful Middle School: This We Believe
Characteristics Crossover

- Comprehensive counseling and support services meet the needs of young adolescents.
- Varied and ongoing assessments advance learning as well as measure it.
- Organizational structures foster purposeful learning and meaningful relationships.

The research on, literature about, and visual representations of multi-tiered systems of support (MTSS) is as diverse as the students we serve. Most succinctly, it is defined as "an overarching framework that typically includes a continuum of prevention and intervention supports to help the whole child be successful in academic, behaviors, and other dimensions such as social/emotion and mental health."[15] MTSS is an umbrella term used to include a variety of services that are provided in schools and considers the intensity and frequency with which they are delivered. It is a more systematic approach that not only includes intervention for academics and behaviors, but also provides a framework for pedagogy, leadership, professional learning, equitable access, and implementation.

For the purposes of this book, we brainstormed our combined understandings and beliefs about MTSS and the best way to capture its function in middle schools. Additionally, we considered how the CSCP should have its own pyramid of interventions that works simultaneously with the academic and behavioral intervention triangles. It was through this process that we deemed MTSS the engine of the train—and trains can't go anywhere without their engine. We see MTSS as a way of doing business and, similar to SEL, not "something else." The planning and careful implementation of MTSS should involve every department and stakeholder in your building. To best help you with the planning and aligning process, we have narrowed the concept to its four major components or focus points.

> ***Expert Advice:*** Take time to develop what counseling interventions can look like and how both direct and indirect services can be implemented at all three levels. School counselors have a plethora of data on and knowledge of students that helps in developing individual plans to support them.

Whole Child

It is unclear when and who coined the term "whole child," but the approach has been around for several decades and likely has its roots in John Dewey's work. In his lecture series before parents and educators in April 1899, Dewey addressed the need to no longer see children as empty receptacles. Instead, educators, working as a community, should want for students "as parents want for their children."[16] "Only by being true to the full growth of all the individuals who make it up, can society by any chance be true to itself. And in the self-direction thus given, nothing counts as much as the school."[17] He further called his proposal the "New Education" where we educate the whole child and remain flexible to their needs, helping them learn more than just lessons but to better understand the life of their community and be able to adapt to social needs. And now, you may ask, how are we still figuring this out in 2023?

In 2007, the Association for Supervision and Curriculum Development (ASCD) introduced its Whole Child Initiative, which was grounded in Maslow's 1943 hierarchy of needs, in order to develop a picture of school that included measures to ensure that each child is: healthy, safe, engaged, supported, and challenged.[18] The introduction of the ASCD framework correlated with the launch of MTSS as a preventative framework and then further codified into law with the renewal of the Every Student Succeeds Act (ESSA) in 2015.[19] These developments resulted in states adopting improvement efforts that include measures well beyond academics and have expanded the roles of schools. Integrating the Comprehensive School Counseling Program is one of the most important pieces to the success of all of these frameworks and meeting the needs of the whole child.

A CSCP addresses the whole child by providing direct and indirect services and interventions across three domains: academic, college and career readiness, and social-emotional.[20] These services can be in any of the three tiers of MTSS and, just like academic interventions, may increase with intensity and duration. Below are just a few examples.

- In the academic domain, the school counselors support all students through the process of helping make course selections for the following year based on their strengths and interests, or how they might work toward high school graduation goals. Additionally, school counselors can support students through small group counseling focused on study skills or stress management.
- In the college and career readiness domain, school counselors collaborate with or provide teachers with career exploration lessons and activities.
- In the social-emotional domain, school counselors meet with students individually or in small groups to work on areas such as self-regulation and coping skills.

When a CSCP is designed to meet student needs through these three domains, the whole child can be addressed. While this is accomplished by a school counselor's direct work with students, the whole child's needs are also supported through collaboration with teachers, staff, families, and the community.

> **COUNSELOR CALL IN**
>
> *A school counselor can be a great asset when supporting a student who is receiving consequences. But if not used thoughtfully by administration, they can actually damage the rapport and trusted relationship.*
>
> —Anonymous

The What: "The Middle School Transportation System"

Team Approach

The Successful Middle School: This We Believe states that "successful middle schools intentionally organize people, time, and space to maximize young adolescents' growth and development" (2021, p. 50). Furthermore, effective teams serve as the foundation for a strong learning community. In *Successful Middle School Teaming,* Jack Berckemeyer defines teaming broadly as "one group, same teachers, same students, same goals!"[21] While he is writing about the teaming concept in middle schools, Berckemeyer's definition is holistically applicable for MTSS as well.

Schools using the team approach to MTSS share a common goal to remove barriers to learning at a systems level. This means that everyone in the school has a hand in ensuring student success. Beginning with our first encounter with students and families all the way through Tier 3 interventions, everyone in the school should share a common purpose of working together to meet student needs. This approach holds true not just for things that happen inside the school walls but also for how we engage families. The Ohio Statewide Family Engagement Center at the Ohio State University provides a wealth of resources for schools to engage families in a variety of tiered practices and strategies to foster a true partnership and team effort while differentiating for the needs of the family.[4]

In collaboration with school leaders, school counselors can set the tone for the team approach to MTSS with a shared purpose statement that is aligned with the school vision and mission. Using the information gathered in the "Collaborative Data Reflection Activity" as a baseline, leaders and school counselors can lead the school in developing a shared understanding of MTSS and its purpose. Given the importance of MTSS—remember, it's the engine that takes your train everywhere—aligning it with school vision and mission will be of the highest importance. In this process, we recommend two key actions:

1. Develop an MTSS team that includes representation from across your school, grade levels, student services, different content areas, administration, and school counseling.

---

[4]*For more about the center visit https://ohiofamiliesengage.osu.edu/

2. Develop a vision/mission or purpose statement for your MTSS team to guide the work and provide commitments for implementation and accountability.

> **PRINCIPAL PERSPECTIVES**
>
> *During my first years of the principalship, I learned what valuable partners our counselors were. It is incredibly important to invite their input on decisions that will impact the educational and emotional well-being of students. The counselors have valuable insight into the needs of students and including their perspective can help decision-makers consider unintended effects of the changes being considered.*
>
> *– Allyson Apsey*

There are several options here with creating an MTSS purpose statement aligned to the school's vision and mission statements. Either way, both serve as public commitments about the work that will be done.

For your purpose statement, we recommend using 1-2-4 Process outlined in "Ways to Reach Agreement on Just About Anything" found in *Successful Middle School Teaming*.

Data-Driven Decision Making

Data-driven decision making is a process by which schools collect and analyze data, turning insights into action. A key component is that the data collected has a purpose and is related either to the school improvement plan or to other initiatives. For MTSS, data should be used to screen, progress monitor, and align multi-tiered

The What: "The Middle School Transportation System"

interventions, ultimately helping the school meet the academic, behavioral, and social-emotional needs of students.

I once heard a colleague say, "if you are collecting data and not doing anything with it, stop collecting it." No truer words were ever spoken. We are effectively using data to guide decisions when we collect the right data, use a data protocol like root cause analysis to review the data, and then turn it into actionable next steps.

When it comes to data-driven decision making, we recommend considering both cause and effect data as well as using the root cause analysis to tackle your biggest decisions. Cause and effect data considers adult behavior (cause) and the results of that behavior (effect). A root cause analysis is an approach to analyzing problems found in data before trying to solve them. Teams are encouraged to identify the problem and ask the question "why?" no less than five times, or use the familiar fishbone diagram. Resulting answers must be something that can be controlled by the organization, not outside forces.

Root Cause Analysis: How to Use the 5 Whys

- Write down the problem. Be specific.
- Begin asking why the problem exists, only including answers that are in your control.
- Once you have asked "why?" five times, you should be at the root cause. If not, keep asking until you have agreement.

Root Cause Analysis: How to Use the Fishbone Diagram

- Write the problem statement in the head of the fish.
- It may be helpful to label larger areas on the fish as you begin to think of causes. Possible examples could be time, schedule, curriculum, partnerships, community, policies.
- In the skeleton of the fish, list possible causes. Consider data sources to back up the statements.
- Ask "why?" as you are listing causes.
- *It may be helpful to label your causes as related to adults or students, and then cross off the ones that are labeled with students.*

Fishbone Diagram

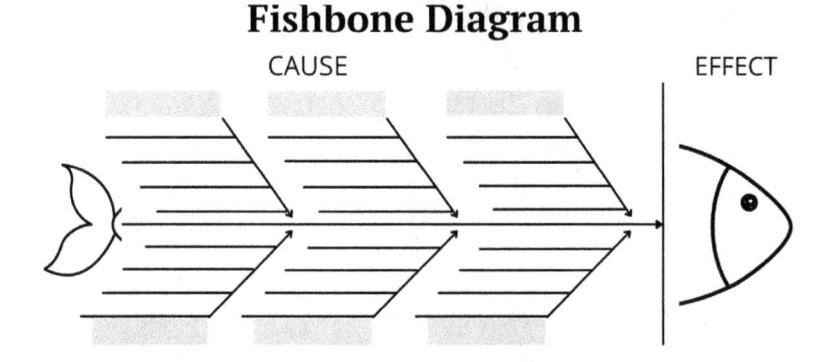

CAUSE → EFFECT

Read the scenario below and work through the process of data-driven decision making.

Scenario – Data-driven decision making. What would you do?
Your school administers an SEL survey two times a year, every year, and has been doing it for several years. Your data consistently, and over time, shows that sense of belonging is lower in your 8th grade than other grades. You have implemented SEL and your schedule includes an advisory period, but you are not seeing the same results in 8th grade as the other grades. Given that increasing belonging is one of your school goals, what will you do?
What other data sources would you review?
What could be the root cause for lower 8th grade data?
Decision or strategy to address root cause

The What: "The Middle School Transportation System"

Collaborative Leadership

Author and lifelong educator Rick Dufour describes collaborative leaders as those "who share authority, empower others, and assess their effectiveness as leaders on the extent to which they create the conditions that result in higher levels of learning–both for students and adults."[22] When we reflect on this in terms of MTSS we consider the "conditions" and break them into policy and practices, professional capacity, and communication and collaboration. We believe it is in this element that MTSS begins to differentiate itself from other intervention initiatives.

Policy and Practices

Leaders work collaboratively with all stakeholders to implement both policies and practices that connect initiatives and create an inclusive and equitable school environment. Note that there is a difference between a policy and a practice.

- A policy is something that has been codified and adopted by the school board.
- A practice is how administration interprets the policy and implements it at the school level.

School teams must be cognizant of the students and communities they serve to ensure that the practices are both systematic and equitable. A truly collaborative system will have checks and balances so that practices are not creating gaps and students are not falling through the cracks.

Professional Capacity

Professional capacity refers to the development of staff to create, grow, lead, and implement MTSS efforts. MTSS is a big undertaking for schools. Principals cannot go it alone. Sharing leadership empowers staff and supports efforts to systematically implement MTSS with fidelity.

Communication and Collaboration

Setting the tone and message for MTSS will fuel your engine. Collaborative leaders plan not only for communication, but also for feedback. Communication should be a circular process where feedback is just as important as the original message. When fully implementing MTSS, leadership must make sure that resources and time are shared in order to fully benefit from the tiered approach. Coordinating an effort like MTSS will require ongoing communication that is fueled by feedback.

In all of these elements, the CSCP plays an integral part. Working collaboratively on the school improvement plan, the school counseling department can inform the needs of students to ensure programming and practices are equitable. School counselors should not only serve on the MTSS team, but also deliver specialized professional development for staff to better understand the social-emotional needs of students and how to meet those needs in the classroom. As shared leaders, school counselors can help communicate the importance of educating the whole child at school, with parents and caregivers, and in the greater community.

CHAPTER 12: BRINGING IT ALL TOGETHER: THE TRAIN IS LEAVING THE STATION

Throughout Section Two, we have provided you with the research base and several frameworks to consider as you design or improve your CSCP. By this point, it should be evident that integrating the CSCP is not as simple as it might seem. So far, you have engaged in several reflective activities for each of the introduced frameworks. We hope these are helpful in deciding how to build your railway. The programming and services delivered by the CSCP should be on equal footing with the focus given to academics and behavior.

Consider everything you have read in this chapter. Most specifically, consider the role of your comprehensive school counseling department in each of these elements of your railway. Take time to reflect on how your school counseling department is currently implementing the CSCP and the role they play in the larger school operations. These reflections should fill the Current Reality section in the exercise on the following page. Then think about how you can integrate the school counseling department, creating goals for implementation. Completing this exercise will help you prepare for Section Three – The How.

The What: "The Middle School Transportation System"

Train	Research and Frameworks	Current Reality	Implementation Goals
Rail 1	SMS, TWB • 5 Essential Attributes • 18 Characteristics		
Rail 2	The ASCA National Model • Define • Manage • Deliver • Assess		
Ties	SEL & CASEL Framework • CASEL 5 • CASEL Settings		
Engine	MTSS • Whole Child • The Team Approach • Data-Driven Decision Making • Collaborative Leadership		

SECTION TWO REVIEW

We're making good progress on our railway; the tracks have been laid and our engine is powered up! Let's review the highlights of Section Two. By now you should have:

1. Reflected on the 5 Essential Attributes and 18 Characteristics of Successful Middle Schools;
2. Completed a current implementation check of the ASCA National Model at your school;

3. Reflected on the current roles of your school counseling staff and evaluated their time spent delivering services;
4. Reflected on your current understanding and beliefs related to social-emotional learning;
5. Completed several activities to create a baseline of SEL implementation at your school;
6. Developed or reviewed the membership of your MTSS team to include creating a purpose statement;
7. Completed a root cause analysis to practice data-driven decision making; and
8. Reflected on your current role of your school counseling program as an embedded entity in your school organization and started implementation goal setting.

Before beginning Section Three, think again about the intricacies of the railway system. For example, railroad crossings and underpasses: without them we would have grave safety concerns and traffic congestion. But with them, both people and trains move efficiently and effectively. The last section will highlight how all facets of the school can work together to achieve better outcomes.

Additional Questions for Reflection

- What assumptions have been challenged in this section as you reflect on the foundation for developing a CSCP?
- If anything in this section is an area of growth for your school, where will you start?
- What additional research or information do you need to gather on topics in this section in order to better understand its function in a successful middle school?
- What is a practice you might change moving forward to support the success of the school counseling program in your school?

Section Three
The How

Section Three

The How
"All aboard!"

SYSTEMATIC APPROACH TO PROGRAMMING AND IMPLEMENTATION

In Section Two, we explored the middle school transportation system including the rails, ties, and engine that tie to foundational documents and frameworks that can shape your school's CSCP and how utilizing all of them can help you best meet the needs of young adolescents. In this section, we will help you bring them together to systematically put the railway components into action as you think about your CSCP.

CHAPTER 13: DEFINING THE SYSTEMATIC APPROACH IN COMPREHENSIVE SCHOOL COUNSELING PROGRAMS

The Successful Middle School: This We Believe
Characteristics Crossover

- Every student's academic and personal development is guided by an adult advocate.
- Comprehensive counseling and support services meet the needs of young adolescents.

In true school counselor fashion, we are going to check in with you at this point in the book. How are you feeling about your understanding of a CSCP and how to integrate it into your school to support students?

> **STOP, THINK, & JOT**

When thinking about a systematic approach to a CSCP, building leadership can rely upon best practices they know to be effective when supporting the efficacy of any other department. Simply put, a systemic approach begins with the standards: looking at data to see where students are, identifying where they need to go, planning how we will help them get there, and assessing along the way. But before looking at any standards or curriculum, start with the "why."

Defining our why sets the foundation to inspire our purpose. In his book *Start with WHY*, Simon Sinek asserts that some organizations start with the "what" because it is the clearest and easiest area to articulate resulting in a product.[1] However, the "why" can be more ambiguous for stakeholders to understand and articulate as it is often tied to personal beliefs. This puts a fine point on the need for vision, mission, or purpose statements to align. Without this alignment, the "how" and "what" can result in opposing directions of what systems and practices are put into place, further stretching school resources and adding the potential for train derailment. Once the "why" is established and aligned, the school counseling department begins the work of the "how."

The Role of Data in School Counseling

The "how" is where effective use of data begins. Effective use of school data is necessary to implement all components of the ASCA National Model. However, data plays a more significant role in MANAGE and ASSESS. In the MANAGE component, the school counseling department is pulling school outcome data to analyze where the CSCP needs to focus services. This data also guides the creation of goals, providing a roadmap for how the CSCP will support student growth. You may also consider longitudinal process data from the CSCP to assess its effectiveness and consider changes that need to be made for the upcoming year. Process data, as defined by ASCA, "is descriptive in nature and communicates what happened during the intervention and who was impacted. This type of data includes but is not limited to the number of students who participated; when the intervention occurred; and the duration, frequency and intensity of the intervention."[2]

Exploring Process Data

As an example, if the school counselor visited classrooms to speak to students about academic planning, the analysis of this process data could look at the timing of the lessons to ensure course selection information is available in time for staffing decisions. Through this process, the school counseling department will determine if there is any additional data that needs to be collected, which could include perception data. Though it should be used with caution, perception data can complement outcome or process data for feedback purposes. A survey given to students can yield important insights; for example, that your students would like more information on time management, but that they would not be open to attending a short-term small group to receive targeted support in this area. This data could be shared in a collaborative team meeting and overlapped with grade-level work completion data, resulting in classroom lessons in time management.

In the ASSESS component, end-of-year data is analyzed to determine "how students are different as a result of the school counseling program" across academic, social-emotional, and college and career readiness.[3] This process can be enhanced by the practices suggested in the next several chapters.

Direct and Indirect Services

As mentioned previously, ASCA recommends a minimum of 80% of school counselors' time be spent in direct and indirect services, with the remaining 20% in program planning (ASCA, 2019). In Section Two, you completed a reflection activity on the roles or duties that school counselors have, are involved in, or are responsible for to help determine how your school counseling staff is using their time. When using intentional, efficient collaborative practices, such as those suggested in this section, not only can school counselors accomplish the 80% goal of direct and indirect services but they are also able to execute those services in a way that works synergistically and systematically with other initiatives and practices in the building and/or district.

> **PRINCIPAL PERSPECTIVES**
>
> I would have wanted to know and understand that the counseling program should go beyond scholars coming to the counselor's office when there was a problem but that counselors should develop a schedule that includes whole class visits, parent workshops, policy advocacy, and help lead the advisory class plan.
>
> – Cedrick Gray

Figure 2 is a sample of a week in the life of a school counselor whose time meets the recommended 80/20 allocation. Though this sample is certainly a simplified version of a week in the life of a school counselor, it shows the possibility of implementing an effective CSCP when time is dedicated to activities and responsibilities that can be tied to accomplishing standard- and data-driven student improvement goals.

The How: "All aboard!"

Figure 2 – A Week in the Life of a School Counselor

Monday	Tuesday	Wednesday	Thursday	Friday
Morning Student Check-ins	Morning Student Check-ins	Morning Student Check-ins	Morning Student Check-ins	Morning Student Check-ins
Blue Team Meeting	Content Team Meeting	Individual Counseling	Career Exploration Class Lessons	Student Mediation
Yellow Team Meeting	Organization Small Group	Content Team Meeting	Data Collection and Program Planning	Data Collection and Program Planning
Lunch	Lunch	Lunch	Lunch	Lunch
Class Lesson Planning	Stress Coping Skills Group	MTSS Meeting	Parent Calls	Career Exploration Class Lessons
Individual Counseling	Classroom Observation	Replying to Parent/Caregiver and Teacher Emails	Small Group Planning	Class Lesson Planning: Review Data and Coordinate Make-up Sessions

Lunch	Direct Services	Indirect Services	Programming

For more ASCA resources on tracking school counselor time, visit schoolcounselor.org

Ultimately, by aligning your CSCP to the ASCA National Model, the program will accomplish a systematic approach to providing services to support student improvement in academic, social-emotional, and college and career readiness. This alignment also moves school counselors to a more proactive role while still allowing them to react to students in crisis.

> **COUNSELOR CALL IN**
>
> *Research indicates that building a positive relationship with students is the first component of a successful counseling relationship. This is reinforced through direct student contact and often compromised when fulfilling indirect disciplinary roles such as lunch duty.*
>
> *-Joe Caldwell*

Expert Advice: Not sure whether your school counseling program is in alignment with the ASCA National Model? Use the evaluation tools on ASCA's website to assess your program, identify a baseline and next steps to ensure your CSCP is effectively serving students and aligned with school and district goals.

CHAPTER 14: THE SCHOOL ADVISORY PROGRAM

The Successful Middle School: This We Believe
Characteristics Crossover

- Every student's academic and personal development is guided by an adult advocate.
- Organizational structures foster purposeful learning and meaningful relationships.

The How: "All aboard!"

The AMLE Glossary of Middle Level Education Terminology defines advisory as "regularly scheduled times when young adolescents have the opportunity to interact with a small group of peers and a teacher-advisor to discuss school and personal concerns." The Glossary of Educational Reform defines advisory as "a regularly scheduled period of time, typically during the school day, when teachers meet with small groups of students for the purpose of advising them on academic, social, or future-planning issues."[4] These combined definitions provide us with a holistic look at meeting the needs of young adolescents through dedicated time with purpose. Advisory is a hallmark of the middle school model and is considered a uniquely middle school structure. While it has many variations, its foundational purpose remains largely the same: create a safe, inclusive environment where students and adults engage in activities that foster relationships and promote health and social well-being. Advisory is designed to optimize the middle school experience and provide any or all of the following:

- A safe place that embraces risk-taking
- An opportunity to practice mutual respect
- A time to connect with a trusted adult
- A space for advocacy and support
- A space to practice kindness and empathy
- A forum for healthy discussion or debate
- A place for goal-setting and self-reflection
- A time for collaboration and cooperation
- A dedicated time for culture-building

When we consider the purpose and structure for advisory, it should be considered a Tier 1 intervention for MTSS. It is designed to be an all-hands-on-deck structure to keep the student-teacher ratio as small as possible. Given this, it would make sense that the planning and implementation of advisory would also include all hands on deck. Unfortunately, due to a variety of reasons, advisory sometimes becomes a stand-alone program that does not receive appropriate professional development, dedicated time in the schedule, required focus and support, and proper planning. Too often, a curriculum is purchased by districts and simply handed to advisors. To combat some of these challenges, we recommend instructional staff and school counselors work collaboratively to create a more responsive advisory program. The CSCP can assist in developing and facilitating any of the following teams to create an advisory program that is designed by your staff specifically for your students.

Advisory Planning Team

The advisory planning team should include representation from administration, school counseling, all grade levels, departments, and other service providers from your building. Aim to be as inclusive and representative as you can. This team is charged with setting the goal and purpose of your program. Much like MTSS and other committees in the school, we recommend a vision/mission or purpose statement that codifies the work of both the advisory team and program. This team acts as representatives of the full staff and should answer important questions about the structure of the advisory period, including:

1. Who teaches/coaches the advisory period?
2. What will the curriculum be?
3. Where will we meet with students?
4. Why is it important to allocate time to advisory?
5. When will it be offered during the day, week, month?
6. How will we evaluate its effectiveness?

The advisory planning team may create a year-long calendar that maps both long- and short-term goals. This team can also help to shape the focus and communications, both internal and external. Lastly, the advisory planning team should seek input for and advise on the ongoing professional development that may be needed for advisors. This will go a long way to ensure that the staff understands the purpose and buys into the program. We recommend that this planning be collaborative with the SEL team and instructional leaders in the building to maximize the benefit of connecting advisory lessons to daily instruction.

SEL Planning Team

Much like the advisory planning team, the SEL team should also include representation from administration, school counseling, all grade levels, departments, and service providers from the building. Additionally, CASEL recommends including out-of-school services, community partners, students, and their families in this group as well. This team might be considered a "sub-group" or separate "work group" of your larger advisory planning team depending on your context or availability of staff. The primary work of this group should be to focus on school-wide or Tier 1 systems and act as experts in SEL for advising, advocacy, and ownership of social-emotional learning.[1]

Instructional Leadership Team

This is where our train avoids the possibility of going off the rails. When we carefully combine the efforts of the advisory team, SEL team, and instructional leadership, our train engineers are less likely to say, "Gee, that town looks exciting, let's turn right and go over there!" The use of curriculum planning calendars has long been best practice including, we hope, also for advisory and SEL. But let's take it one step further: If we know that curriculum mapping already exists, and we have a goal of embedding SEL into instruction, it makes the most sense to have all of that planning in one place. Inevitably, there will be specific standards, lessons, and strategies that lend themselves to richer and more applicable SEL opportunities than others, and planning with those in mind will make the most of this process. Therefore, this planning is a more collaborative approach rather than just one team doing the work. Let's explore this further in the final chapters.

CHAPTER 15: THE TEAM APPROACH

The Successful Middle School: This We Believe
Characteristics Crossover

- Every student's academic and personal development is guided by an adult advocate.
- Curriculum is challenging, exploratory, integrative, and diverse.
- Instruction fosters learning that is active, purposeful, and democratic.
- Organizational structures foster purposeful learning and meaningful relationships.

---

[1] For more information on assembling, roles, and responsibilities of the SEL team, visit casel.org.

One of the most distinctive structures of middle grades schools is teaming: two or more teachers working together to meet the needs of an identified group of students. *The Successful Middle School: This We Believe* notes that teams provide the foundation for a strong learning community and can positively influence a "student's sense of belonging, social bonding, and connectedness." In the perfect world, schools have both interdisciplinary and collaborative teams. Interdisciplinary teams share students in common where collaborative teacher teams share content in common—sometimes referred to as professional learning communities. Regardless of whether it is an interdisciplinary or collaborative team, we propose that including the school counseling staff as an equal partner is essential. It is by having this voice and perspective at the table that teams can truly see instruction holistically with focus on all three of Bloom's domains: cognitive, affective, and psychomotor.

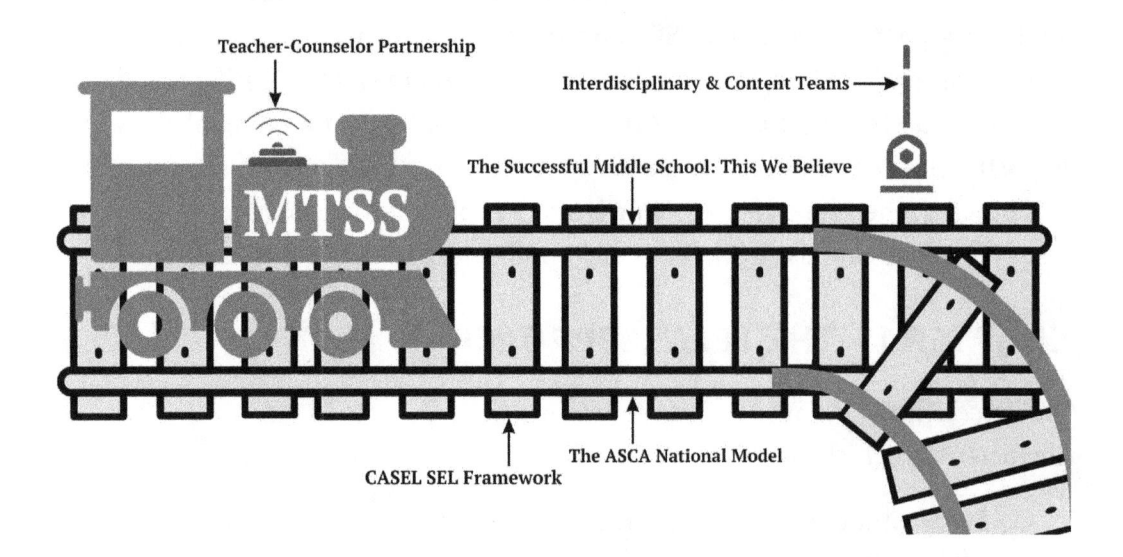

Interdisciplinary Teams

Creating interdisciplinary teacher teams consists of combining staff to share students in common. Teams are interdisciplinary in nature and help create a feeling of family within the school. These teachers work together to create an experience

The How: "All aboard!"

for students that is connected academically, socially, and personally. These smaller structures within the school help students make the developmental leap from elementary to middle school.[5] Interdisciplinary teams provide teachers with the opportunity to plan across multiple disciplines and coordinate assessment. The smaller design of teams also allows teachers to form relationships with students to foster positive culture and help build community. When teachers know their students well, they are able to provide more relevant experiences that are built on their interests and include their voice. Thus, it is beneficial for school counselors to be included in the conversation and not just a part of the agenda that includes "student concerns."

Interdisciplinary teams have great synergistic power in that they can discuss student strengths and needs across multiple disciplines. They can plan for opportunities that include academic, social-emotional, and behavioral activities that bring students together and foster connections. Interdisciplinary teams also have the responsibility of team management which provides the window to plan for communication, family engagement, student conferences, and intervention when students need assistance. When school counselors are considered part of the interdisciplinary team—not simply those who observe team meetings—the team's perspective broadens and becomes more inclusive. Further, the presence of the school counselor provides a more holistic implementation of MTSS given that the team is typically the first line of defense in addressing student needs.

While many team meeting minutes include agendas and management items, we suggest a more robust approach that serves as a running record for the interdisciplinary team to communicate with collaborative content teams. Discussion topics may include: student data trends, implementation of interventions across disciplines, and parent/caregiver communications. Figure 3 is a sample from the Team Discussion Template (included as Appendix D), outlining a holistic approach to team meetings that documents where the school counselors can support.

Figure 3 – Team Discussion Template Sample

Topic	Notes	Actions & Follow Up
Good News		
Looking Ahead: Dates, Meetings, etc.		
Student Services		
Collaborative Data Documentation		
Student Connections		
Parent Connections		
Technology Needs/Issues		

Through discussion, with action items for follow-up, the team can delegate responsibilities to ensure that there is a systematic approach to interventions and services. At the bottom of the template, you will notice a space for links to Collaborative Instructional/Behavioral Support Plans which we will introduce in the last section of this chapter. We recommend that you link this to every meeting template to maximize your staffing and resources.

Appendix D: SMSCP Team Discussion Template

Team Name:	Date:

Members Present	Team Norms

Team Information - Helpful Links
Consider linking pertinent information so that members can stay up to date and have easy access. Below are some sample ideas that you might want to include.

Special Education /504 Schedule	Special Education Accommodations	Data Collection	Field Trip Forms	Request for School Counselor Observation
504 Accommodations	Locker Combinations	Master Calendar	Morning Duty Chart	Computer Cart Reservations

Topic	Notes	Actions & Follow Up
Good News		
Looking Ahead: Dates, Meetings etc		
Student Services		
Collaborative Data Documentation		
Student Connections		
Parent Connections		
Technology Needs/Issues		

Links to Collaborative Instructional/Behavioral Support Plans

Created by Ann Perez and Elise Caldwell. The Successful Middle School Counseling Program 2023. © Association for Middle Level Education.

School counselors are an asset to interdisciplinary teams as they offer additional perspectives and expertise, and can conduct non-evaluative observations to assist teachers in addressing student needs. When students are having difficulty, it often happens in more than one class; this can be easily troubleshooted by the team. But what happens when the issue is isolated, appears to be more of an environmental issue, or the team is unable to adequately address the issue? Here, the school counselor can provide a combination of direct and indirect services.

Direct service is when the school counselor can meet with the student to discuss the concerns or further probe into the root cause. Indirect service is when the issue is addressed through means of observation and consultation. When school counselors visit a classroom for an observation, their specific training and skills assist them in analyzing the environment to identify factors that might inhibit learning. Data gathered during the observation can assist the team in collaboratively planning with the school counselor on how to best approach the situation. Figure 4 provides a sample request form school leaders can use to start this process (also included as Appendix E).

For this observation, we recommend a quick turnaround so that, ideally, the data can be shared at the next team meeting, providing the team with the timeliest information. The school counselor will communicate findings with the team and share ideas to address the concerns.

Collaborative Content Teams

In order to meet the academic, social, and personal needs of young adolescents, staff should have common planning time to facilitate professional learning communities or collaborative teams. In the same way that Interdisciplinary teams share students, collaborative content teams share content. Combining these two organizational structures allows schools to make the most of their schedule and meet the needs of students.

The key core belief of professional learning communities is that all students can succeed at high levels.[6] To achieve this goal and ensure high levels of learning, collaborative teams engage in rich discussion that is focused on learning and centered around curriculum, instruction, assessment, and intervention. The team should take time to discuss and answer the following questions:

The How: "All aboard!"

Figure 4 – Student Concern Request for School Counselor Observation

Teacher Name:	Date of Request:
Student Name:	
Presenting Concerns (check all that apply)	**Description:**
☐ Academic	
☐ Behavioral	
☐ Social Emotional	
Previous Interventions from Team:	
Observer Name:	Date of Observation:
Observer Notes:	
Follow Up and Action Plan:	

87

- What is it that we want students to know and be able to do?
- How will we teach it?
- How will we assess it? How will we know it is working?
- What will we do for students who don't respond? How will we prepare for those who already demonstrate proficiency?

Here are two additional questions to help teams tap into the power of student voice and active engagement:

- How does the instructional plan facilitate student agency?
- How will we ensure that instructional strategies are equitable and engaging for all students?

> **COUNSELOR CALL IN**
>
> Like teachers, each counselor has had very different approaches and pedagogy when counseling students. My predecessor modeled how important the principal/counselor relationship is to improving student achievement. If this trusted, respectful, and collaborative relationship doesn't exist. It would be challenging to achieve the school's mission/vision.
>
> -Wendy James

While you likely have your own template for collaborative content meetings, we want you to consider a different way to see this. If we are to meaningfully embed SEL competencies into our instruction we must consider the school counselor's input as it relates to curriculum, instruction, assessment, and intervention. The school counselor can provide ideas on how to embed SEL into the curriculum as

The How: "All aboard!"

well as help with action planning. In The Collaborative Team Conversation Minutes Template (Appendix F) you will notice spaces on each side of the questions for teacher and school counselor input. This allows for the intended discussion to take place, but now with deliberate input from the school counselor. After each question is answered, the team can then discuss the action plan, roles, responsibilities, evidence, and timelines. Figure 5 provides a sample from the full template.

Figure 5 – Collaborative Team Template Sample

Teacher Input	Curriculum	School Counselor Input
	What do we want students to know and be able to do?	
Learning Targets		

Here is what it might look like with counselor input.

Teacher Input	Curriculum	School Counselor Input
Standard: Analyze how an author develops and contrasts the points of view of different characters or narrators in a text.	*What do we want students to know and be able to do?*	**SEL Competency of Social Awareness:** Ability to understand the perspectives of and empathize with others, including those from diverse backgrounds, cultures, and contexts.
Sample Learning Targets • Students will be able to identify varying points of view in a story with supporting evidence from the text. • Students will be able to understand that points of view can be different. • Students will be able to ask and answer questions to clarify viewpoints. • Students will be able to understand other perspectives or points of view. • Students will gain greater insight into perspective taking.		

Let's now consider the two additional questions that we suggest adding to your collaborative content teams and how the school counselor can support the team in this effort.

Student Voice How does the instructional plan facilitate student agency?	Through identifying points of view and understanding that not everyone agrees, students will be learning how to develop their own point of view. Students will also be able to identify with characters in their reading or engage in perspective taking while getting to know the characters.
School counselor input or support needed	
The school counselor can provide insight into potential reasons a student or group of students may have a difficult time with perspective taking. They can also support by providing strategies to scaffold the language for a student to access skills of perspective taking at a lower developmental level.	

Relevance How will we ensure that instructional strategies are equitable and engaging for all students?	Students will be reading and discussing texts that reflect their own identities as well as others. Discussion in the classroom will be structured using protocols that allow all voices to be heard.
School counselor input or support needed	
School counselors can support teachers in identifying and acknowledging their unconscious bias that may be embedded in the lesson. School counselors can serve as a resource for engaging students in self-reflective questions that explore identity awareness.	

The How: "All aboard!"

The collaborative content team, in conjunction with the school counselor, would complete the conversation by embedding and choosing the most appropriate instructional practices. As mentioned previously, this collaborative effort brings together Bloom's three domains, resulting in a more holistic approach to the instruction. Just like the Team Meeting Template, we suggest linking the Collaborative Instructional/Behavioral Support Plans, introduced below.

The Switchyard: Combining Your Efforts

A railroad switchyard is where cars are shifted from one track to another by means of a system of switches. In the same way, collaboration between interdisciplinary and content teams helps us switch our efforts to the best available strategy to help students. In our experience, we have witnessed the overwhelming desire to help students by throwing every intervention at them to see which one works. Unfortunately, the incorrect intervention will not get the desired results. To carefully tease out the true issues, the teams must consider all the data, including specific student needs and context, and then decide the best way to intervene and who should take the lead. Through this process, teams can make efficient use of their time and efforts while meeting the most pressing needs of the student.

Creating the Collaborative Instructional/Behavioral Support Plan: Part 1

The Collaborative Instructional/Behavioral Support Plan (Appendix G) can guide teams through the process of identifying the issue's root cause, choosing the correct intervention strategy, and determining who has the primary responsibility for implementing. Let's take an in-depth look at this type of plan.

Figure 6 – Review Data, Presenting Issue, Choose Strategy and Define Expected Outcomes

Student Name:			Team/Grade:	Date:
Presenting Issue	Data Considered	Root Cause	Strategy for Intervention	Team/Person Responsible

Expected Outcome(s)

Expert Advice: *This process can be initiated by whichever team has identified a presenting issue with a student. However, a representative who is part of both teams is responsible for communicating the need for the plan to the other team. The interdisciplinary team is the most ideal for keeping track of the records as they will regularly meet to discuss students' needs and be able to identify response and growth across multiple settings. The content team can provide subject area expertise and insight into the most effective instructional strategies for intervention.*

During this part of the plan creation, the team will determine the implementation conditions which includes how, when, and how often the strategy will be implemented. The team will then decide what kind of data to collect, the type(s) and frequency. Because this is a holistic approach that includes the input of school counseling, we recommend collecting both quantitative and qualitative data.

The How: "All aboard!"

Figure 7 – Conditions and Data

Implementation Conditions	Data Collection and Monitoring
How, when, and how often will the strategy be implemented?	What data will be collected? How will it be collected? With what frequency will it be collected? (include qualitative and quantitative data)

Creating the Collaborative Instructional/Behavioral Support Plan: Part 3

After 4–6 weeks of implementation, the team should review the effectiveness of the intervention and decide if any changes need to be made. They can keep a running record of this through multiple entries on the plan. We recommend including a rationale for keeping, modifying, and referring for additional support to help others know where to pick up or leave off in the planning process.

Figure 8 – Plan Review

Next Step: 4-5 week review process	☐ Keep current interventions	☐ Stop or modify interventions	☐ Refer for additional support
Date of Review:	Rationale for decision:		

After the team has implemented, reviewed, and modified the plan, if the student is still not responding to intervention the team would then refer to the MTSS team for further review. Throughout this process, and as part of the MTSS team, the school counselor plays a vital role in communicating the efforts and interventions that have been implemented and further brainstorming how to best meet the needs of the student.

Appendix G: SMSCP Collaborative Instructional/Behavioral Support Action Plan

Student Name:			Team/Grade:		Date:	
Presenting Issue	**Data Considered**	**Root Cause**	**Strategy for Intervention**		**Team/Person Responsible**	
(Example: Comprehension) *(Example: Blurting in Class)*		*Based on the data considered, what are possible root causes of the presenting issue?*	*(Example: Teacher guided, sequencing of events from text)* *(Example: Daily behavior chart)*			

Expected Outcome(s)

Implementation Conditions	Data Collection and Monitoring
How, when, and how often will the strategy be implemented?	What data will be collected? How will it be collected? With what frequency will it be collected? (include qualitative and quantitative data)

Next Step: *4-6 week review process*	☐ Keep current interventions	☐ Stop or modify interventions	☐ Refer for additional support
Date of Review:	**Rationale for decision:**		

Created by Elise Kenney-Caldwell and Ann Perez. The Successful Middle School Counseling Program 2023. © Association for Middle Level Education.

The How: "All aboard!"

CHAPTER 16: CONNECTING EVERYTHING: WORKING SMARTER

The Successful Middle School: This We Believe
Characteristics Crossover

- A shared vision developed by all stakeholders guides every decision.
- Every student's academic and personal development is guided by an adult advocate.
- Varied and ongoing assessments advance learning as well as measure it.
- Leaders demonstrate courage and collaboration.

In an age of education where resources are often scarce, it feels like each new initiative is one more "thing," making the life of an educator more difficult. What if the approach was to not pile everything on that we know works for students, but to weave each into a tapestry where they all work together? This tapestry would create strength with each woven layer, allowing educators to respond freely to the ever-changing landscape of the students walking through their doors.

> **COUNSELOR CALL IN**
>
> *Involving school counseling practices at the ground level of planning for student success helps not only accomplish goals for students, but allows school counselors, teachers, administrators, and staff to all learn from each other and develop new skills.*
>
> -Debbie Ondrus

The goal of this chapter is to help you evaluate your current systems to identify areas that overlap or might need attention. Through this process, you can identify duplicative efforts and reallocate your resources to be more efficient. By clearly outlining goals, identifying the who and the what, your team can decide which efforts should be placed in which departments and which should be collaborative. By analyzing how your current systems work together, the goal is to not add one more thing to everyone's plate, but to work smarter.

Figure 9 is a Systems Crosswalk (Appendix H) that you can use with any of the groups in your school to ensure that you are maximizing your time, staffing, and resources. This exercise is designed to help evaluate Tier 1 systems from a whole school lens and should be done collaboratively with at least one member of any team, department, or committee in your school organization.

Figure 9 – Systems Crosswalk and Reflection

What is the primary goal?	Each system or team in place should have a primary goal. Most educators today desire to have more time: more time for planning, collaborating with peers, or even just to eat their lunches. Therefore, it is crucial that the goal of a system or team is clear for it to be a valuable use of time.
What is in place?	What current systems, processes, practices, and/or expectations are in place for this team, department, or committee? Listing current practices helps to further define the purpose of the work and who is responsible. It also helps to identify possible areas for efficiency.

What data is being used/ collected?	This section helps teams determine how much and what types of data is being collected and to what end. In our experience, it is possible to have a lot of data and no good information. The team should list what data is being used consistently for decision making and planning. This section will help to determine the reliability of that data, highlight which groups use similar data, and outline opportunities for collaboration to meet student needs. *Expert Advice: Though this is a Tier 1 exercise, this look at data across settings can be used for Tier 2 and 3 intervention and is another opportunity for a comprehensive intervention for those students who need more targeted support or enrichment.*
Who is currently implementing?	This question will identify which parties are a part of the various systems and teams. This question can reveal where there is overlap and can be helpful when answering the final question. It also aids in understanding of how various stakeholders in the school community are being utilized and if there might be opportunities to involve additional stakeholders or staff to support the variety of teams and systems in place.
Where could collaborative practices occur?	Here is where you begin to see your school start working "smarter, not harder." This question is meant to gain insight into which efforts are being duplicated and which can be used in more than one system or team. This question can be answered with collaborative practices that are already occurring in your building: there is certainly no need to remove any positive practices that are in place. There might be new insights for improvement with this exercise where those existing positive collaborative practices are in place.

Figure 10 demonstrates how the questions might be answered in regards to the school counseling program.

Figure 10 – School Counseling Systems Crosswalk

	What is the primary goal?	What is in place?	What data is being used/collected?	Who is currently implementing?	Where could collaborative practices occur?
CSCP	*Support student academic, social-emotional, and college and career readiness growth*	*ASCA National Model aligned Comprehensive School Counseling Program*	*Outcome: attendance, grades, and discipline Process: Use of time and services provided*	*School counselors, Director of Counseling*	*School counselors attend interdisciplinary and content team meetings*

As your teams work through the process and resources in this chapter, we hope you are noticing where your efforts overlap and how working collaboratively can not only save you time but allow you to better meet the needs of your students as well. This process should also illustrate the many ways that school counselors can offer their unique training and advocacy for students to improve your current instructional and academic processes.

APPENDIX H: SYSTEMS CROSSWALK AND REFLECTION

Team, Department, or Committee	What is the primary goal?	What is in place?	What data is being used/collected?	Who is currently implementing?	Where could collaborative practices occur?
School Counseling Program					
SEL Team					
Interdisciplinary Teams					
Content Teams					
MTSS					
Other					

Created by Elise Kenney-Caldwell and Ann Perez. The Successful Middle School Counseling Program 2023. © Association for Middle Level Education.

SECTION THREE REVIEW

You have arrived! Completing Section Three means your train has made it safely to its destination. Let's review the highlights of Section Three. By now you should have:

1. Discussed how you systematically use data in your Comprehensive School Counseling Program;
2. Reviewed your team approach to interdisciplinary meetings;
3. Reflected on how to involve the school counselor in gathering classroom data to assist in planning for interventions;
4. Reflected on how to involve the school counselor in collaborative instructional planning in order to truly embed SEL competencies into instruction;
5. Reflected on how both interdisciplinary and content teams working together can better create Instructional/Behavioral Support Plans; and
6. Completed the Systems Crosswalk to realize areas of overlap and create efficiencies in your staffing and resources.

Additional Questions for Reflection

- What assumptions have been challenged in this section as you reflect on how counselor time is used?
- What assumptions have been challenged in this section as you reflect on how counselors should be involved in teachers' planning process?
- How will you work to ensure that advisory is not the sole responsibility of the CSCP?
- What is a practice you might change moving forward to support the success of the CSCP in your school?

CONCLUSION

"There is only one way to eat an elephant: a bite at a time."

– Desmond Tutu

As you have read this book, you have been presented with information, taken opportunities for reflection and analysis, and been asked to challenge existing ideas of how to approach collaboration with your CSCP. Desmond Tutu says it best on approaching systemic changes: start small. Making one or a few changes at a time will allow you to not only implement them with fidelity, but to also have a clearer picture of the effectiveness of that change. Start with the Systems Crosswalk: the best way to know where you are going is to first understand where you have been.

Like a train moving across the country, the path of the change process is not linear. Implementing change and enhancing opportunities for collaboration is a circular process of planning, action and analysis, and adjustment. A key relationship to cultivate in this process is that between administrator and school counseling leadership. Meeting regularly with school counseling leadership is valuable to ensure that the ideas and processes laid out in the book are implemented with both the school and CSCP's vision and mission, as well as school counseling professional standards. Leadership is one of the themes that runs throughout the ASCA National Model and this book provides opportunities for school counselors in your buildings to positively contribute in those roles to accomplish shared goals for all students to grow.

In Section One, we discussed the "who" of Comprehensive School Counseling Programs.

We are hoping that you took time to see that while middle school is a team effort, each entity has a role in supporting the success of the CSCP. In this section, you were able to begin the collaborative process of determining how the school counseling program will be a part of your school improvement plan that is guided by a shared vision and mission. The activities in this section will set you up for success in ensuring that the CSCP is a partner in meeting the unique needs of the young adolescents you serve.

In Section Two, we explored the "what" of foundational documents and structures to help drive the collaborative work of your CSCP. The 5 Essential Attributes and 18 Characteristics of Successful Middle Schools paired with the ASCA National Model provide the rails to keep your train on the tracks. Powered by the engine of MTSS, and held together by standards and SEL competencies, your middle school train is built for efficiency and safe transport. Through the exercises in this section, you should have a good baseline for how your school counselors should be spending their time and are cognizant of changes that you need to make or areas of growth for your program and school.

In Section Three, we learned how to create a systematic approach to CSCP programming and implementation. We laid out the many structures in middle schools designed to support students and explored the idea of bringing them together to better meet their needs. The school counselor plays a vital role as a participant in each of these structures with unique perspective, experience, and training. We

The How: "All aboard!"

hope that by completing the exercises in this section that your team identifies the power of collaboration and realizes areas of duplication to make the most of your time, staffing, and resources.

Throughout this book we explored the elements of implementing a Comprehensive School Counseling Program tied directly to the 18 Characteristics of Successful Middle Schools and the ASCA National Model. *The Successful Middle School: This We Believe* helped us along the way to identify key components of the middle school concept and how to make them come alive in our schools. We hope this book helps you create or refine a successful middle school counseling program.

The steam begins to puff and the whistle blows; your train is ready to leave the station. Jump aboard, the middle school journey is an amazing one when we work together to the benefit of students. You won't want to miss the ride.

APPENDICES

APPENDIX A: COLLABORATIVE DATA REFLECTION ACTIVITY

Discussion Topic	Suggested data points to consider	Principal	School Counselor
Roles/Responsibilities How does the school counseling program or specific counselors fit into the strategic plan?	Goal data from the previous year		
Demographics: Do school policies and practices meet the needs of all students?	Enrollment data Special populations Course enrollment Intervention data		
Academic Achievement Data: How can the school counselor support this and at what Tier?	Grades Assessments		
Discipline Data: How do school trends match with data from the counseling department?	Perception Data Needs assessment SEL surveys		
Attendance Data: How can program services and interventions from school counseling assist in this area?	Tardies Absences Extreme cases of truancy Transiency data		

Created by Elise Kenney-Calwell and Ann Perez. The Successful Middle School Counseling Program 2023 © Association for Middle Level Education

APPENDIX B: ASCA Annual Administrative Conference

AMERICAN SCHOOL COUNSELOR ASSOCIATION — Annual Administrative Conference

School Counselor _____   School Year _____

After completing the school data summary, I have identified the following data priorities:

_____
_____
_____

Based on these data priorities, I will address the following goals as listed in the annual student outcome goal plan templates:

Annual Student Outcome Goals	
1	
2	

School Counselor Use of Time
A minimum of 80% of time is recommended for direct and indirect student services and 20% or less in program planning and school support.

Use of Time from Previous School Year
Based on two use-of-time 5-day calculators from previous school year (attached)

Direct Student Services	Indirect Student Services	Program Planning and School Support	Non-School-Counseling Duties
%	%	%	%

Use-of-Time Plan for Current School Year
Indicate your planned time allocations for this school year

Direct Student Services	Indirect Student Services	Program Planning and School Support	Non-Counseling Duties
%	%	%	%

Updated, June 2021

APPENDIX B: ASCA Annual Administrative Conference

Ratio and Caseload

The American School Counselor Association recommended ratio is one school counselor per 250 students.

Ratio: One School Counselor Per _____ Students

Caseload defined by:
- [ ] Alpha Assigned: Last names beginning with: _____ to _____
- [ ] Grade Level: Students in grades: _____
- [ ] All Students in Building
- [ ] Other: _____

Program Implementation Plan to Address Priorities

Attach the following documents for review and discussion during the conference:

- Classroom and Group Mindsets & Behaviors Action Plan
- Closing-the-Gap Action Plan
- Annual Calendar

Advisory Council

The school counseling advisory council will meet to provide feedback and input on the school counseling program.

Fall Meeting Date:	
Spring Meeting Date:	
Proposed Members: *(names and stakeholder position)*	

Professional Development

I plan to participate in the following professional development based on annual student outcome goals and my School Counselor Professional Standards & Competencies self-assessment.

Date(s)	Topic	Cost

Updated, June 2021

APPENDIX B: ASCA Annual Administrative Conference

School and District Committees and Professional Work		
Group	Time Commitment	School Counselor's Role

Budget Materials and Supplies

Materials and supplies needed: _____

Annual budget: $ _____

School Counselor Availability/Office Organization

The school counseling office will be open for students/parents/teachers from _____ to _____

My hours will be from _____ to _____ (if flexible scheduling is used)

The career center will be open from _____ to _____

Other Staff and Volunteers

Role/Responsibility	Person Assigned (no signature required)
School Counseling Department Assistant	
Attendance Assistant/Clerk	
Data Manager/Registrar	
College and Career Center Assistant	
Other Staff	
Volunteers	

Signatures of school counselor and administrator must be within the first two months of school.

Updated, June 2021

APPENDIX B: ASCA Annual Administrative Conference

School Counselor Signature	
Administrative Signature	
Date Conference Held & Template Signed	
First Day of School	

Updated, June 2021

Appendix C: Student Needs Assessment

Last Name: First Name:

Grade Level:

In the table below, select all that apply around each topic.

I would like more information regarding the following **PERSONAL** concerns:

	I would like someone to speak to me individually	I would be interested in being in a group around this topic	I would be interested in having a class lesson on this topic	I am not interested in this topic
Identifying and coping with uncomfortable emotions				
Handling stress				
Substance Use/Abuse				
Grief/Loss				
Communicating with family				
Friendship (making, keeping and communicating))				
Equity or diversity in school				
Other:				
Other:				

Created by Elise Kenney-Calwell and Ann Perez. The Successful Middle School Counseling Program 2023
© Association for Middle Level Education

In the table below, select all that apply around each topic.

I would like more information regarding the following **SCHOOL** concerns:

	I would like someone to speak to me individually	I would be interested in being in a group around this topic	I would be interested in having a class lesson on this topic	I am not interested in this topic
Organization				
Communicating needs or questions with teachers				
Time management				
Studying for tests or quizzes				
Understanding class expectations for work				
School transitions				
School mindset/motivation				
Understanding and following expected behaviors				
Other:				
Other:				

Please list any other concerns or information you would like your school counselor to know about you:

Created by Elise Kenney-Calwell and Ann Perez. The Successful Middle School Counseling Program 2023
© Association for Middle Level Education

Appendix D: SMSCP Team Discussion Template

Team Name:		Date:

Members Present	Team Norms

Team Information - Helpful Links
Consider linking pertinent information so that members can stay up to date and have easy access. Below are some sample ideas that you might want to include.

Special Education /504 Schedule	Special Education Accommodations	Data Collection	Field Trip Forms	Request for School Counselor Observation
504 Accommodations	Locker Combinations	Master Calendar	Morning Duty Chart	Computer Cart Reservations

Topic	Notes	Actions & Follow Up
Good News		
Looking Ahead: Dates, Meetings etc		
Student Services		
Collaborative Data Documentation		
Student Connections		
Parent Connections		
Technology Needs/Issues		

Links to Collaborative Instructional/Behavioral Support Plans

Created by Ann Perez and Elise Caldwell. The Successful Middle School Counseling Program 2023. © Association for Middle Level Education.

APPENDIX E: STUDENT CONCERN REQUEST FOR SCHOOL COUNSELOR OBSERVATION

Teacher Name:	Date of Request:
Student Name:	
Presenting Concern *(check all that apply)* ☐ Academic ☐ Behavioral ☐ Social Emotional	**Description:**
Previous interventions from Team:	
Observer Name:	Date of Observation:
Observer Notes:	
Follow Up and Action Plan:	

Created by Elise Kenney-Caldwell and Ann Perez. The Successful Middle School Counseling Program 2023. © Association for Middle Level Education.

Appendix F: SMSCP Collaborative Team Conversation Minutes Template

Grade/Content:	Date:

Members Present

Norms:
Roles:

Teacher Input	Curriculum	School Counselor Input
	What do we want students to know and be able to do?	

Learning Targets

Teacher Input	Instruction	School Counselor Input
	What instructional or behavioral strategies will we use?	

Strategies + Cause & Effect data to be discussed:

Teacher Input	Assessment	School Counselor Input
	How will we assess it? How will we know if it is working?	

Action Plan

Teacher Input	Intervention	School Counselor Input
	What will we do for students who don't respond? How will we prepare for those who already demonstrate proficiency?	

Action Plan

Created by Elise Kenney-Caldwell and Ann Perez. The Successful Middle School Counseling Program 2023 © Association for Middle Level Education.

Appendix F: SMSCP Collaborative Team Conversation Minutes Template

Student Voice How does the instructional plan facilitate student agency?	
School Counselor input or support needed	

Relevance How will we ensure that strategies are equitable and engaging for all students?	
School Counselor input or support needed	

Team Reporting/Feedback

What is the action plan for the team? What needs do you have? Do you have anything that needs to be reported to the building leadership?

Parking Lot

Links to Collaborative Instructional/Behavioral Support Plans

Created by Elise Kenney-Caldwell and Ann Perez. The Successful Middle School Counseling Program 2023 © Association for Middle Level Education.

Appendix G: SMSCP Collaborative Instructional/Behavioral Support Action Plan

Student Name:			Team/Grade:		Date:
Presenting Issue	**Data Considered**	**Root Cause**	**Strategy for Intervention**		**Team/Person Responsible**
(Example: Comprehension) *(Example: Blurting in Class)*		*Based on the data considered, what are possible root causes of the presenting issue?*	*(Example: Teacher guided, sequencing of events from text)* *(Example: Daily behavior chart)*		

Expected Outcome(s)

Implementation Conditions	**Data Collection and Monitoring**
How, when, and how often will the strategy be implemented?	What data will be collected? How will it be collected? With what frequency will it be collected? (include qualitative and quantitative data)

Next Step: *4-6 week review process*	☐ Keep current interventions	☐ Stop or modify interventions	☐ Refer for additional support
Date of Review:	**Rationale for decision:**		

Created by Elise Kenney-Caldwell and Ann Perez. The Successful Middle School Counseling Program 2023. © Association for Middle Level Education.

APPENDIX H: SYSTEMS CROSSWALK AND REFLECTION

Team, Department, or Committee	What is the primary goal?	What is in place?	What data is being used/collected?	Who is currently implementing?	Where could collaborative practices occur?
School Counseling Program					
SEL Team					
Interdisciplinary Teams					
Content Teams					
MTSS					
Other					

Created by Elise Kenney-Caldwell and Ann Perez. The Successful Middle School Counseling Program 2023. © Association for Middle Level Education.

About the Authors

Dr. Ann McCarty Perez is a passionate educator with 26 years of experience working in schools to improve processes and outcomes. She has been a middle school teacher, high school assistant principal, middle school principal, and central office administrator for curriculum, instruction, and assessment. She is well versed in state and federal programming and data driven decision making. In her various roles she has implemented curriculum reviews and writing activities, program and process reviews, MTSS and responsive instruction, student behavior modification plans and PBIS, coordinated projects to reduce truancy, increased student achievement and closed gaps, provided services for at-risk students, and collaborated with parents to create school community. Her experience includes a variety of settings to include urban, sub-urban, and rural schools.

As a presenter and facilitator, Dr. McCarty Perez has helped school leaders with vision and mission, scheduling, equity and courageous leadership, implementation of MTSS, power standards, and using Professional Learning Communities to increase teacher capacity and improve instructional outcomes. As a school and district leader, she has demonstrated results of closing achievement gaps and improving outcomes for all students through continuous improvement efforts and strategic planning. In addition to her work in K-12 education, Dr. McCarty Perez has been an adjunct professor at George Washington University where she worked with aspiring school leaders on supervision of instruction. She most recently authored the Successful Middle School Schedule as the first companion guide in the series for The Successful Middle School: This We Believe.

The Successful Middle School Counseling Program

Elise Kenney-Caldwell has served students for over 20 years in a variety of settings beginning with her career as an instructional assistant at Bonnie Brae Elementary School. Elise always knew that her path would take her to serving students and her passion for the mental well-being of students would be realized in her work as a school counselor. In her current role as Counseling Director, Elise Kenney-Caldwell serves students, school counselors, teachers and parents through the Comprehensive Counseling Department at Williamsburg Middle School in Arlington, Virginia. She is responsible for overseeing the counseling department, evaluating school counselors, and working collaboratively with the school administration to coordinate the master schedule, 504 administration and services. Her work across schools and districts has included the design and implementation of MTSS, coordinating SEL efforts, and contributing to career exploration activities for school and community. She has both coordinated and facilitated efforts for gap closing and providing after school assistance for students.

In addition to her work in the counseling office, Elise established a Peer Mediation program for 8th grade students and has mentored students through coaching on the soccer field. Her work has also included contributing to the Virginia Department of Education Career Exploration Modules to meet new standards.

As both school counselor and counseling director, Elise Kenney-Caldwell has worked collaboratively with parents to provide in school and out of school programming for parents and students. She has hosted parent book clubs and educational programs to help elementary and middle school parents navigate the system and variety of needs of middle school students. Elise has specific training in the IB Middle Years Programme, Functional Behavior Assessments, Responsive Classroom, MTSS, Behavior Management, and Reading in the Content Area.

Ann McCarty Perez and Elise Kenney-Caldwell have known each other for close to two decades and have had the privilege of working side by side to serve middle school students. Ann has served as an administrator and Elise as professional school counselor. While they no longer work together, their strong belief in doing the best for students has continued to be a bonding force in their professional lives and friendship. Their combined passion and expertise for middle school students has been brought together in this text to help schools realize the power of the comprehensive counseling program.

References

SECTION 1

1. ASCA National Model: American School Counselor Association (2019). The ASCA National Model: A Framework for School Counseling Programs, Fourth Edition. Alexandria, VA: Author.
2. ASCA National Model: American School Counselor Association (2019). The ASCA National Model: A Framework for School Counseling Programs, Fourth Edition. Alexandria, VA: Author.
3. McCarty Perez, A. (2022). *The successful middle school schedule*. Association for Middle Level Education.
4. Ibid.
5. Bishop (2021).
6. Jordan, C. (2022). Developing productive school counselor–principal partnerships. *Professional School Counseling, 26*(1c). https://doi.org/10.1177/2156759X221134669
7. Hattie J. (2023). *Visible learning : the sequel : a synthesis of over 2 100 meta-analyses relating to achievement* (First). Routledge.
8. Hattie J. (2012). *Visible learning for teachers : maximizing impact on learning*. Routledge.
9. Bandura, A. (1977). Social learning theory. Englewood Cliffs, NJ: Prentice Hall.
10. Hattie, J. (2023). *Visible learning: The sequel: A synthesis of over 2,100 meta-analyses relating to achievement*. Routledge
11. Bloom, B. S. (1956). Taxonomy of educational objectives: Cognitive and affective domains. New York: David McKay.
12. CASEL (2015). CASEL guide: Effective social and emotional learning programs: Middle and high school edition. Chicago, IL: CASEL. Retrieved from CASEL.org
13. Bachman, H. & Boone, B. (2022). A multi-tiered approach to family engagement. Retrieved from https://www.ascd.org/el/articles/a-multi-tiered-approach-to-family-engagement
14. Quaglia R. J. & Corso M. J. (2014). *Student voice: The instrument of change*. SAGE Publications.

15. Ibid.
16. Reeves, D. (2022). *Fearless schools: Building trust, resilience, and psychological safety.* Archway Publishing.
17. ASCA National Model: American School Counselor Association (2019). The ASCA National Model: A Framework for School Counseling Programs, Fourth Edition. Alexandria, VA: Author.

SECTION 2

1. Association for Middle Level Education. (n.d.). *AMLE strategic plan 2022–2026: A vision for the future of AMLE and middle level education.* Retrieved from https://www.amle.org/strategic-plan-2022-2026-a-vision-for-the-future-of-amle-and-middle-level-education/
2. (HBR, 2011) Merchant, Nilofar (2011) Culture Trumps Strategy, Every Time. Harvard Business Review. Retrieved from https://hbr.org/2011/03/culture-trumps-strategy-every
3. ASCA National Model: American School Counselor Association (2019). The ASCA National Model: A Framework for School Counseling Programs, Fourth Edition. Alexandria, VA: Author.
4. Ibid.
5. Goodman-Scott, E., Betters-Bubon, J., Olsen, J. A., Donohue, P., & Young A. (2020). *Making MTSS work.* American School Counselor Association.
6. Bishop (2021).
7. ASCA National Model: American School Counselor Association (2019). The ASCA National Model: A Framework for School Counseling Programs, Fourth Edition. Alexandria, VA: Author.
8. Ibid.
9. Ibid.
10. Ibid.
11. The Committee for Children. (2023). *What is social-emotional learning?* https://www.cfchildren.org/what-is-social-emotional-learning/
12. Positive Action. (n.d.). *What is SEL? Social-emotional learning defined & explained.* Retrieved from https://www.positiveaction.net/what-is-sel
13. Hattie, J. (2023). *Visible learning: The sequel: A synthesis of over 2,100 meta-analyses relating to achievement.* Routledge
14. Fisher D. Frey N. Quaglia R. J. Smith D. & Lande L. L. (2018). *Engagement by design : creating learning environments where students thrive.* Corwin Literacy.

References

15. Goodman-Scott E. Betters-Bubon J. Olsen J. A. Donohue P. Young A. & American School Counselor Association. (2020). *Making mtss work* (First). American School Counselor Association.
16. Dewey, John (1907) The School and Society: being three lectures by John Dewey supplemented by a statement of the University Elementary School. Chicago: University of Chicago Press.
17. Ibid.
18. Maslow, A. H. (1943). A theory of human motivation. Psychological Review, 50, 370–396.
19. Schaffer, G. E. (2023). Multi-Tiered systems of support: A practical guide to implementing preventative practice. Sage Publications. Thousand Oaks, California.
20. ASCA National Model: American School Counselor Association (2019). The ASCA National Model: A Framework for School Counseling Programs, Fourth Edition. Alexandria, VA: Author.
21. Berckemeyer, J. (2022). *Successful Middle School Teaming.* Association for Middle Level Education.
22. Buffum, A. G. (2008). *The collaborative administrator: Working together as a professional learning community.* Solution Tree.

SECTION 3

1. Sinek, S. (2019). *Start with why: How great leaders inspire everyone to take action.* Penguin Business.
2. ASCA National Model: American School Counselor Association (2019). The ASCA National Model: A Framework for School Counseling Programs, Fourth Edition. Alexandria, VA: Author.
3. ASCA National Model: American School Counselor Association (2019). The ASCA National Model: A Framework for School Counseling Programs, Fourth Edition. Alexandria, VA: Author.
4. Glossary of Educational Reform retrieved at : https://www.greatschoolspartnership.org/resources/glossary-of-education-reform/
5. McCarty Perez (2022).
6. DuFour R. DuFour R. Eaker R. Many T. W. & Mattos M. (2016). Learning by doing : a handbook for professional learning communities at work third edition (a practical guide to action for plc teams and leadership) (3rd ed.). Solution Tree Press.